PRIME

PRIME

The state or time of greatest vigour or success in a person's life
"You're in the prime of life."

Olive Strachan

Copyright © 2023 Olive Strachan
All rights reserved.
ISBN: 9798873329076

DEDICATION

I dedicate this book to my husband Errol George Strachan. We met when I was nineteen and he was twenty-four and forged a life together, building our own family tree which currently stands at a family of ten with our children, Rhia Boyode and Ricky Strachan, together with their spouses, Anthony Boyode and Seryana Strachan, and our four beautiful granddaughters, Mya, Zendaya, Sophia, and Ezrah.

My life has been rich with your love and support, all we have achieved we have achieved together, believing in each other, and through all that we have had to face we stand strong, shoulder to shoulder, never giving up, looking to the future, and providing a legacy for our children.

Thank you, Errol, for being by my side through the forty-two years of our life together. The red stone of our Ruby anniversary symbolises romance, devotion, and passion — all the wonderful things that being married to you represents. I know that I am blessed to have you in my life; I cherish, love, and appreciate you.

In the words of Bob Marley "In high tide or low tide, I'll be by your side."

FORWARD

I am thrilled to have the pleasure of introducing this book to you. *Prime* is the sequel to *The Power of You*, also published by Olive Strachan, a role model to so many, with a truly remarkable ability to help great people become exceptional and bring great people together for connection and inspiration.

Olive has touched the lives of so many through her books, workshops, events, and personal coaching business, fully embracing the now, no matter what the situation, for as long as I can remember, and who predictably also inspired me by being a great role model.

I am personally excited about this book's topic and how relevant it is of the times; as I write this it's the annual celebration of the Windrush generation, recognising how ordinary people did extraordinary things.

This book is both an inspiration and frustration. An inspiration because you will read a collection of personal experiences and achievements of an incredible woman, and a frustration because of the experiences of racism that still exist in our society today.

The way Olive has interwoven anecdotes and personal references with tips and stories will educate and enhance your understanding of women in business, women's health, the importance of inclusion and belonging, and building resistance. A lot of Black British and Caribbean history is covered here too, an extraordinary fusion of history, literature, health and wellbeing, business, and travel.

It is my privilege to present my darling mother's second book to you, living her best life, and most definitely in her prime!

Rhia Boyode
Director of People & Organisational Development
for Shrewsbury and Telford Hospital NHS Trust

CONTENTS

CHAPTER 1 The Early Years - where I come from 1
CHAPTER 2 England: the land of milk and honey 7
CHAPTER 3 Maintaining our Caribbean culture 14
CHAPTER 4 Creating a new life 18
CHAPTER 5 Time to grow up! 22
CHAPTER 6 Becoming a wife and mother 28
CHAPTER 7 Building a life together 33
CHAPTER 8 A resilient marriage 38
CHAPTER 9 Prime for business 40
CHAPTER 10 Nurturing aspirations and fulfilling professional dreams 49
CHAPTER 11 Say no to the "pause" 53
CHAPTER 12 Life's rich tapestry 58
CHAPTER 13 And so the adventure begins 66
CHAPTER 14 Making the transition 71
CHAPTER 15 Reverse culture shock 79
CHAPTER 16 Reflecting and taking stock 90
CHAPTER 17 Rediscovering my Prime 98
CHAPTER 18 Success is never achieved alone 104
CHAPTER 19 From dream to reality – working in Dominica 109
CHAPTER 20 The next step – professionally speaking 112
CHAPTER 21 Inspiring Footprints 114
CHAPTER 22 Living my prime! 115
CHAPTER 23 Full circle 117
APPENDIX Inspiring footprints 120
ACKNOWLEDGEMENTS 129
About the Author 131

INTRODUCTION

My first book, *The Power of You*, chronicled my working life as a Black female entrepreneur and all the challenges I faced and how I overcame them.

This book is the story of my life, from leaving the island of Dominica at six years old and travelling on a ship to England with my mother and sister, then meeting my father for the first time; my school days and growing up in Blackburn, Lancashire, during the late 1960s and 70s; the hurdles we had to overcome, as the only Black family in the area where we lived, navigating our new life in the UK whilst facing racism and discrimination. The book also takes you on a journey of Black culture, encompassing our food and traditions. I share with you meeting my husband, getting married and building a life together, which meant living apart for many years whilst we both pursued our careers.

It spans motherhood and childrearing and how I balanced being a wife and mother, my career in the recruitment industry, and then opening a successful training consultancy and working in over twenty-five countries. The book also highlights key events that had a significant impact on me including the Manchester bombing, the Windrush disaster, Brexit, and the Covid pandemic.

After spending fifty years in England, I returned to Dominica permanently in October 2020 at the height of the pandemic, naively thinking that because I was born in Dominica I would fit in right away! I left everything that I was familiar with behind, my children, grandchildren, friends, and clients. Some of these relationships spanned over forty years. I found it problematic at first and needed time to adjust to my new surroundings, and I share my experience of how I re-evaluated my life by starting again, exploring new avenues, and creating a life with purpose in a new environment.

This was also at a time when I thought I would slow down and retire but on the contrary, it has proven to be one of the most exciting times of my life. I have had to start again and conquer new challenges but in the process I discovered a renewed vigour for life.

I began my career in the recruitment industry, working for Brook Street Bureau in Manchester, when I was a young mother with a six-month-old baby. From day one I realised that I loved the work, and the feedback I received confirmed that I had a skill for matching the right staff to the right organisations. Soon after, I exceeded my sales target to the extent that I raised one of the largest revenues ever recorded at Reed Employment in Manchester at that time. I was young, in my twenties, married to my lovely husband, had a job that I loved – and I thought I was in my prime.

Then when I established my own business, Olive Strachan Resources, in my late thirties, I employed staff, won my first international contract - and I thought I was in my prime!

In my fifties I completed my master's degree in human resource management and became the first Black female branch Chair of the Chartered Institute of Personnel and Development (CIPD) for the Manchester branch. I thought, that's it, I have reached the pinnacle of my achievements! Then in 2019 I was awarded the MBE by King Charles, then Prince of Wales, for my contribution to Exporting and Business, and again I thought, that's it, I've exceeded my expectations - I have definitely reached the prime of my life!

In my sixties I was awarded Chartered Companion of the CIPD and my company won the Training and Coaching Enterprise Vision Award. Not least, I started a new life in the Caribbean which really pushed me out of my comfort zone, but I found my feet and now work globally with Dominica as my base. I am continuing to pursue a career that feeds my heart, my soul, and my intellect.

When the realisation came to me that actually I was in the prime of my life *now*, I wrote and posted a short article on LinkedIn entitled "When are we in our prime?" I said that I was looking forward to my seventies because I feel that in life, we have not just one, but many primes. My LinkedIn post received 242 likes, 114 comments and four reposts and sparked a great deal of discussion. The conclusion was that our prime is whenever we want it to be! This feedback, together with the feeling of optimism and anticipation that I was experiencing, inspired me to write this book.

This is the story of how I navigated the move to the Caribbean, experienced a sense of loss bordering on depression and then came through that experience to feel happy again, carving out a new life with a sense of purpose and pleasure.

In this book I also explore what is it like for someone returning to the place they were born after a prolonged absence, moving to the UK in the 1960s where we did not feel welcome, growing up in a place where you will always be seen as "the other" and not quite belonging. When I first arrived in the UK as a child, we lived in a small northern town called Blackburn in Lancashire. In 1967 it was quite acceptable for a complete stranger to say, "Why don't you go back to where you came from?" When we would go home crying to our mum and dad, they would comfort us by telling us that we did belong somewhere, and that Dominica was our home. This gives Caribbean people of my age unrealistic expectations about the welcome they will receive when they return to the Caribbean. Moving away for over fifty years separates you from your roots, because you grow to reflect the place where you live. I have a Northern English accent, as I spent my early years in Blackburn and then later lived in Manchester for over thirty-eight years. To a Caribbean person who has been based there most of their life, I am not recognised as one of them. In Dominica, they call me "the English woman."

It was not an easy transition, and I had many moments of just wanting to go to the airport and return to all that was familiar, but having gone through that experience and come out the other side, I wondered how many other women had gone through this self-same experience, and how did they overcome the feeling of not belonging or fitting in?

I arrived in Dominica at the age of fifty-nine, feeling that my best years were behind me and ready to retire, because that was what most of my friends were contemplating at the time. Many of my friends in the UK have started working part-time or given up their work life to become full time carers for aging parents or to provide support with grandchildren. Starting again in later life creates all sorts of obstacles, some that society creates and some that you create yourself as learned behaviour.

I have decided that my prime is the here and now - it's when I decide it is! I hope that by sharing my journey it will help others who may be thinking about moving, or who have done so but have not found it easy to achieve happiness and fulfilment.

CHAPTER 1
The Early Years - where I come from

"A people without the knowledge of their past history, origin and culture is like a tree without roots."
Marcus Garvey

I can't start a book about my prime without taking you through the early years of my life because we are the sum total of our experiences. Reading my story it will become clear that up until later in my life I was not really in control of my own life. My parents emigrated from Dominica to the UK, taking me with them. This wasn't something that I could control. Later in my thirties I was married with two children, had gained some expertise in my career, returned to university to complete my studies, and suddenly felt that I was in control of my own destiny. But I will start at the beginning.

When anyone asks me where I was born, I say "Dominica" but frequently it is confused with The Dominican Republic, which shares the island of Hispaniola with Haiti to the west, in the Greater Antilles archipelago of the Caribbean region, and where the official language is Spanish.

Dominica, on the other hand, is an island country in the Windward Islands of the Lesser Antilles in the eastern Caribbean, lying between the French islands of Guadeloupe to the north and Martinique to the south, with the Atlantic Ocean to the east and the Caribbean Sea to the west. A member of the Commonwealth since independence in 1978, its official name is The Commonwealth of Dominica. The island is 29 miles (47 km) long with a maximum breadth of 16 miles (26 km) and the capital and chief port is Roseau. The official languages of Dominica are English and Creole, or French Patois ("Kwéyòl").

My husband, Errol, is Jamaican but he fell in love with Dominica in part because of its spectacular, lush landscape. It is known as The Nature Island of the Caribbean and in July 2022 Dominica was ranked No 1 on the Travel & Leisure

World's Best Awards List of Top Islands in the Caribbean, Bermuda, and Bahamas.

A special part of Dominica's great natural beauty is its spectacular range of high forest-clad mountains, which runs north to south, broken in the centre by a plain drained by the Layou River, which flows to the west. The highest points are Mount Diablotins at 4,747 ft (1,447 m) and Mount Trois Pitons at 4,670 ft (1,424 m). Having lived here for over two years I have found there is so much more to see and enjoy. From the lush beauty of Freshwater Lake at just over 2,500 ft above sea level, and the largest of Dominica's four lakes, it is cool, with a mist hanging over it (it always reminds us of visiting Scotland), to the famous twin waterfalls at Trafalgar Falls. I could go into tourist mode but suffice to say that if you enjoy natural beauty such as lakes, waterfalls, hiking, whale watching, etc, then Dominica is the place to visit.

Dominica is made up of ten administrative regions called parishes (all named after an apostle or saint). I was born in a village called Castle Bruce, which is a village on the east coast and the largest settlement in St David's Parish. This is where my mum's family are from, and the family name is St. Rose. My sister Liza and I were born here, whilst my two other sisters, Susan and Sharon, were born in the UK. My mum, Althea St. Rose, met and married my father, Augustine Collaire, in the late 1950s and moved to live in La Plaine, just further south.

Pierre Colaire – a local hero

My father's family is from Case O' Gowrie, La Plaine, and my sisters live in Case O' Gowrie to this day, where the family home is located. It wasn't until just a few years ago that I became aware that my great, great grandfather was a local hero and there is a monument to him in Case O' Gowrie. Here is an article from the Government of the Commonwealth of Dominica by Dr. Lennox Honeychurch about Pierre Colaire (at that time the family surname was spelt with one 'L' rather than two).

Division of Culture

by Dr. Lennox Honeychurch

"Born at La Plaine in the mid-nineteenth century, Pierre Colaire represents the determination of the small farmer to survive, fighting against the pressures put upon them by the powerful planter interests.

Except for a few enlightened people such as Imray, the large plantation interests held sway, seeking to maintain dominance of agriculture by restricting the growth of the new peasantry. This was done by making it almost impossible for potential smallholders to buy crown lands and by imposing land and property taxes which would force them to leave their subsistence plots and work on the estates for cash so that they could pay taxes. By driving the smallholder back onto the estates, the planter interest hoped to maintain control of labour at a time when there was growing shortage of labour in Dominica. The first test in the battle between the two opposing interests came when Pierre Colaire, a smallholder at La Plaine, refused to pay the tax imposed on his property. As an example, the governor summoned the British Royal Navy warship "HSM Mohawk" to go to La Plaine with policemen and marines to force the eviction of Colaire from his Property. A group of villagers from as far as Delices assembled in protest and were shot at by the police and marines, killing four people.

There was a great political upheaval as a result: local parliamentarians protested to the British government, a commission of inquiry was instituted and eventually the hated tax laws were repealed. The consequences of Pierre Colaire's action in the end was the recognition of the small farmer as the key to Dominica's economic future, rather the inefficiencies of declining estates, and the redirection of agricultural policy in Dominica to meet the needs of the small farmer. He stands as a hero who paved the way for social and economic changes in landholding and labour for modern Dominica."

Reading this article I felt a mixture of sorrow and pride; sorrow because of the impact being evicted from their home must have had on the family but pride that my great great grandfather, Pierre Colaire, was strong and stood up for what was right. I have been to see the Pierre Colaire Monument erected in memory of the event and the four persons who lost their lives. It was erected less than a hundred yards from the actual site of Pierre Colaire's house and it does give me a feeling of belonging. I have always been a strong and resilient woman and now I know some of where it originates from.

Dominica's Lime Factories

My parents were Althea (nee St. Rose) and Augustine Collaire, known as Sonny Boy, or Gus. When I asked my mum how they met she said that they were both working at the lime factory in Dominica. My dad insisted that it was the sight of Mum's long legs that were the attraction! I was born into a family of tall women—apart from me. My mum and three sisters range from 5ft 9 in to 6 ft tall, and I am only 5 ft 4 in. Often, when I was visiting Dominica, my mum would take me with her to visit friends and they would look at her with a puzzled frown and ask, "Who is this then?" Mum would say, "She's Olive, the one who lives in England." Then they would look at me and say, "She doesn't look like you and she is very short!" Mum would retort "She looks like her father, and she is short, just like him." I used to feel slightly inferior, because of the discrepancy in height between me and my sisters, but after a few visits I found it hilarious. I would just wait to see who would say it first! Strangely enough, when I first met my husband I was wearing six-inch heels and he insists that he thought I was much taller than I am and that I tricked him. Well good things come in short packages, that's what I say!

I had no idea that at one point Dominica was one of the biggest producers of limes in the world. As part of my research into my parents and their history I found this interesting article on Wikipedia which describes the lime factories of Dominica:

"In 1753, James Lind discovered that consuming citrus fruits cured people affected by scurvy, a disease rife throughout the British Navy, whose seamen often went weeks without eating fresh produce. Limes were preferred to all other citrus fruits, not because of higher vitamin C, but because they were easier to preserve.

From 1795, it became normal practice throughout all long voyages within the Royal Navy, for sailors to receive a daily ration of lemon or lime juice. This quickly gave rise to the nickname "limeys" amongst non-British sailors, which arises in the early 19th century. The preservation of the fruit juice was usually done through the addition of 15% rum.

Lauchlan Rose (1829–1885), a ship chandler in Leith, began a process for preserving lime juice in 1865 and patented this method to preserve citrus juice without alcohol in 1867. He had realised that preserving the juice with sugar rather than alcohol opened the product up to a far wider market.

The first factory producing lime juice was set up as L. Rose & Co. on Commercial Street in Leith, Scotland in 1868. This was located adjacent to the Old East Dock built during the Napoleonic War. This aided both the supply of limes (which do not grow in the UK), and its proximity to what was then Scotland's principal harbour for the Royal Navy. The limes at this time largely came from Dominica in the West Indies. In 1893, Rose purchased plantations there to ensure his supply."

Reading this article has given me some insight into Dominica's past and also my parents' experience of meeting each other and working together. They met and married in the late 1950's and had my sister, Elizabeth Collaire, known as Liza, in 1959, and then me in September 1961. They were not together very long before my father was offered the opportunity to go and work in England, a chance not to be turned down as in those days England was seen as the land of milk and honey. So it was that in 1961 my father left my mum with my sister, who was just eighteen months old, and me on the way. I didn't meet my father until I was six years old, when we finally went to England. Before she died, I asked my mum if she considered not going to England after such a long separation. She pointed out that because her mother died when she was four years old she never really attended school and a lot of her knowledge came from the school of life. Mum's work experience was working in the lime factory and with a lady who ran her own launderette; Mum said that her hands used to be red raw with washing clothes by hand. The opportunity to start anew and give her daughters a better chance in life meant that there was no other choice to make. I thanked Mum repeatedly for taking that chance; it's because of her foresight and vision for her daughters that I am where I am today.

My sister and I were the lucky ones because at least we had our mother with us. There are many stories and articles published about the "Barrel Children", whose parents migrated abroad from the Caribbean, leaving their children in the care of others. The barrel refers to the blue or brown shipping container barrels that are posted back to the Caribbean containing anything from food stuffs to clothes, books, shoes, etc. These children are often left in the care of relatives or friends for extended periods of time; it can take two to ten years or more to satisfy the legal, financial and immigration requirements of countries like the United States, for example, and some barrel children never see their parents again. An article on NBC News in December 2017, by Melissa Noel, entitled *Jamaica's barrel children often come up empty with a parent abroad* discusses the effect separation can have on children throughout the years, and says that what can't be shipped in those barrels is emotional nurturance. As part of my research for this book I spoke to my husband, Errol Strachan, who was brought up by his grandmother whilst his parents established themselves in the UK. His mother visited and sent money and barrels with clothes and foodstuffs, but he didn't actually leave Jamaica to live with his parents and other siblings until he was 16 years old. Although Errol felt he missed out on the family unit in England he had aunties and uncles not much older than he was, so he had playmates and grew up in a loving household. The great Greek philosopher Aristotle once said, "Give me a child until he is seven and I will show you the man." This applies to my husband, because a lot of his values and beliefs come from his grandparents in Jamaica. The person who he refers to constantly and with whom he had an unshakeable bond was his grandmother, Claris Harrison. She lived to be 102 years old and proudly displayed her letter from Queen Elizabeth II on her 100th birthday.

My father, Augustine Collaire, was the youngest of ten children and was not able to complete his education because his father became blind, a disease which he also inherited. Having to leave school at an early age meant that my father did not have any qualifications and found it difficult to find work on an island with limited possibilities. Dominica's economy is dependent upon agriculture, which is intermittently destroyed by hurricanes. Attempts to diversify have had some success, with a growing tourism industry and a small offshore financial sector. Being offered the chance to escape to a better life in England must have been a tempting offer indeed!

As part of my research as to why so many young men from the Caribbean immigrated to England I explored The National Archives of the UK and in particular a section called "Bound for Britain" looking at post-war 1945 – present. It says:

"Between 1947 and 1970 nearly half a million people left their home in the West Indies to live in Britain. In March 1947 the Ormonde set sail from Jamaica to

Liverpool to bring people hoping for a better future. Later that year, another ship, the Almanzora set sail from Southampton. The Empire Windrush later docked on the River Thames in Tilbury on the 21st June 1948 with 1027 passengers.

The West Indies consists of more than twenty island countries and dependencies in the Caribbean, including Jamaica, Barbados and Trinidad. The people who travelled from these islands changed the face of modern Britain. They were British citizens with the right to enter, work and settle here if they wished.

Looking to give their children a better chance in life, some came to work for a while, save money and return to the Caribbean. Many were responding to the British Government's call for workers in the transport system, postal service and health service. Britain was a country devastated by war and needed workers to help restore the post war economy. Some of those who came were returning servicemen from the Second World War, recruited from Britain's colonies in the Caribbean. From 1944, West Indian women served in the Women's Auxiliary Air Force and the Auxiliary Territorial Service in Britain. From 1944-1945, nearly 5,500 West Indian RAF servicemen came to Britain."

This document gives me so much clarity as to why my father chose to immigrate to England. The British Government requested young Caribbean men to come to Britain, making it possible for them to find work. Luckily for my sister and myself, only my father left to work in England and my mother remained with us.

After six years of being apart my father sent tickets and we joined him in England. He was working and had bought a house in Blackburn, so it seemed logical for us to join him there. Both my parents agreed that for the good of the family, moving to England was the best thing to do.

CHAPTER 2
England: the land of milk and honey

My memories before arriving in the UK are hazy. My sister has a very sharp memory of her early life but for me everything comes into focus when I boarded the ship to the UK. I remember being dressed in a crisp cotton dress and white ankle socks, my hair in two pigtails with white ribbons. It was 1967 and I was on a ship bound for England. My mum suffered from seasickness, which must have caused her some anxiety. She couldn't lock us in the cabin with her all day, so we were allowed to play on deck. I remember having lots of fun and enjoying the trip and recall other passengers and crew being kind and indulgent, as we were not the only children on board.

We arrived in the UK in winter, and I saw snow for the first time. It was strange, touching this cold, white substance. I remember a strange man picking me up and as I turned to my mum in alarm, my Mum said, "Olive, this is your father." In later years, my dad would comment that there was an unshakeable bond between me, my sister and our mum and I think he was right. Those early, formative years when there were just the three of us meant that we had formed a close-knit team which was still there right up to her death on 18 November 2021. Dad was an excellent father, he was a provider and worked hard to make sure that we always had whatever we needed, but my mum was my compass, my guiding light. To this day I always try to follow her standards and live up to her expectations of me.

Our house was a terraced house, two up and two down with an outside toilet, typical of that era. The streets outside were cobbled, very much like in the popular British soap, *Coronation Street*. At the back of the house, we could see the railway line. Often when I was bored, I would imagine that I was one of *The Railway Children*, from the book by Edith Nesbit which was made into a film in 1970, and I would wave to the people in the railway carriages as they passed. The passengers always waved back with a smile on their faces, and I imagine they found it a bit incongruous to see a Black little girl waving at them from a house in Blackburn, Lancashire!

Blackburn did seem cold and gloomy to a child that was used to the sunshine but the person who suffered the most was my mum. At least my sister and I went to school and were out of the house all day. My mum had no friends to talk to and spent all day, every day, at home. She found the long dark nights depressing and couldn't get accustomed to the interminable, dark winters. If we examined her symptoms with a modern lens, we would probably say that she was suffering from Seasonal Affective Disorder (SAD), which is a type of depression related to changes in seasons which begins and ends about the same time every year. Mum was always happier in summer.

My first memory of when we arrived was when we went into what was then called "the front room", a room never used by the family but kept in pristine condition for visiting guests, and as a rule we were never allowed to enter. However, on arrival my father led Liza and I into the front room and gave each of us a piggy bank, which is a small plastic money box. He then pointed to the skirting board where he had painstakingly placed shinny pennies, each one touching, all around the room. We were amazed and proceeded to collect those shiny pennies and put them into our piggy banks. It took us a while and gave our parents an opportunity to catch up with each other.

Compared to the Caribbean sunshine, Blackburn was dark and gloomy, and very, very cold, especially in winter. Liza and I were a novelty in Blackburn; I don't remember seeing any other Black person anywhere. We definitely stood out! We attended St Alban's Roman Catholic primary school and my school days were relatively happy. However, we were the only Black children in the whole school and there were many challenges. Every day someone would ask me about my skin colour, the most frequent question being "Does it come off?", as well as wanting to know if I was that colour because I was dirty, and was I black all over? Each morning my mum would plait my hair and put ribbons in, and every afternoon I would return home with my hair a complete mess. This was because everyone wanted to touch my hair and exclaim about its texture and would run their hands through it. My mum was furious and would insist that I ask them to stop, but with so many children it was impossible. I am not a naturally confrontational person so I just put up with it. I was a bit of a joker and a people pleaser so I got by, but Liza was the serious one and would not tolerate anyone treating us poorly, and as my big sister she defended and protected me. It is difficult growing up in an environment where you are the odd one out. Soon our family grew from four to six, with the birth of my sister Susan in 1968 and then Sharon in 1970. My father had always wanted a son but had four daughters instead, a son was not to be.

It was strange at first, having to defer to two parents instead of just one. We soon discovered that our parents had very different personalities. My father was a flamboyant, fun loving, work hard play hard kind of guy, whereas my mum was more serious and measured, a disciplinarian, good at long term planning. Luckily for me, I had two loving parents who were extremely bright, despite neither one of them having received much formal education. Both my parents were self-taught when it came to developing their skills but they encouraged us to get a good education; my father invested in the Encyclopaedia Britannica to help expand our knowledge and arranged for us to have a tutor to help us with our studies, and Mum came to every school parents' evening. They were both determined to see us thrive in our new home.

The issues I faced were generally outside of my home: school, the media, just walking down the street. On television there was never anyone who looked like me. There were the American films where the Black person had to roll their eyes and speak in a slow drawl that made my toes curl, or where the first person to die was always the Black man. At the time there was a television sitcom called "Love Thy Neighbour"; we were so pleased when it first appeared on our television set, but it was so racist and negative that in the end we stopped watching it. What made us proud were people like Moira Stewart CBE presenting the BBC News, whose mother, Marjorie Gordon, was born in Dominica; Sir Trevor McDonald OBE, another BBC news presenter also with Caribbean heritage; and of course, Sir Clive Lloyd and the West Indies cricket team. As a Black man living in the UK my dad did not have much to boast about or feel proud of, every day was a mental fight to maintain his dignity and self-respect. I do remember the days when the West Indies won at cricket, his body language would change, he would stand just that little bit straighter, with his chest out, and go off to work with a spring in his step. My father worked for a company called Feniger & Blackburn, no longer in operation. He worked hard to support us and eventually my mum gained part-time employment, which meant that she made friends and started to carve out a life of her own.

My father had the ability to create a fun environment wherever he went. Come the weekend, after a full week's work, he would press his suit - because no one else could press his clothes to his satisfaction, those creases in his trousers had to be as sharp as a knife edge - bathe, put on his suit and some aftershave and go out, often to meet his friend, James Nelson, and would end up at the pub. Sometimes we were allowed to accompany him, and whilst sipping my orange juice I would observe other men coming into the pub. They would all greet my father with "Hello Gus". Later he would go home and place bets on the horses, sometimes allowing me or my sister to choose the winning horse. If it won, we would get some of his winnings. Friday night was takeaway night when we would have Chinese food, or fish and chips from the chippy.

At primary school most of our teachers were nuns. Sister Mary Magdalene was in charge. I am not sure about her role but if there was an issue we were always asked to go and see her. She was a very firm disciplinarian and I remember her smacking me with the ruler on numerous occasions, trying to curb my boisterous nature. For anyone who knows me, it is clear that it had no impact whatsoever on my personality! I recall a history lesson where we were discussing the kings and queens of England and after we had discussed Henry VIII and his six wives, I put my hand up and asked the history teacher about my history as a Black person. He looked at me in complete consternation and then pointed to a picture of a slave ship on the wall. It displayed black people in chains, lying like sardines in a can and covered in detritus. I felt like someone had thrown a bucket of cold water over me. We had just been looking at kings and queens in their beautiful gowns, wearing gold crowns, sitting at a table eating game. That was the history of most of my fellow classmates, but mine was a horrific story that made me feel ashamed. If we move forward to the present day, I often speak at events about the issue of Race, specifically about my lived experience as a Black person growing up in the UK. After one of my presentations a teacher, an attendee of the event, gave me some feedback. He had not been aware of the impact he was having on Black children due to his lack of knowledge around Black history and his inability to signpost them to information that could feed their curiosity. He said that listening to my speech had given him valuable insight and he would make some immediate changes to how he addressed Black children when they asked questions about their history. To me this is a small step towards changing the way in which Black history is perceived.

Another instance that sticks in my mind was when I was accused of stealing. I remember we had a young teacher; she had long hair, wore a mini skirt and those long boots that were in fashion in the 1970's. She seemed very nice, and we all liked her. One day she was walking past my desk and she commented that I smelled nice. I thanked her and smiled, and she asked me what scent I was wearing that smelled so nice, and I told her that it was *Mum* antiperspirant, a brand favoured by my mother. She then said that the fragrance was suspiciously like a bottle of perfume which had been stolen from her and asked me, in front of all my classmates, if I had stolen her perfume? Naturally I denied it because I hadn't a clue what she was talking about. She then told me that in order to prove that I had not stolen her perfume I should go home and bring the antiperspirant that I was wearing as evidence that I had not stolen her perfume. At that time, my father worked on the night shift and was asleep at home all day, so when I banged on the door he came and opened it, a little bleary eyed, and asked what I was doing home from school so early? When I explained what had happened, he was incandescent with rage. He quickly freshened up and marched me back to school; I remember he walked so fast that my little legs couldn't keep up with him. He charged into the classroom and told the teacher what he thought of her and I remember there was a lot of shouting. I never saw that teacher again. But I learned that as a Black child you could be picked on for no good reason apart from the colour of your skin. Luckily, both my father and mother explained to me about racism and taught me that I was to always hold my head up high and believe in myself.

I left primary school and became a pupil at John Rigby School in Blackburn, now Our Lady & Saint John Catholic College. I really enjoyed my time at secondary school. I made some lovely friends and had some inspirational teachers. One of the teachers that stands out in my memory is Mr Dunn, a short man, always dressed in a suit, with a military bearing. He commanded respect from both the girls and the boys although there was a lot of laughter and fun during his lessons in Commerce. He taught with knowledge and humour. When exam time came around, I hardly needed to revise, Mr Dunn's excellent teaching meant that I retained a great deal of the information he taught. To this date I remember a Latin phrase he taught us during one of his lessons, *caveat emptor*, the principle that the buyer alone is responsible for checking the quality and suitability of goods before a purchase is made. There were also children from diverse backgrounds in my class, children from India and Pakistan, so although I had always felt different from the herd, now I was not the only one. Another family came to live in Blackburn from Bradford, James and Maureen Nelson and their children, and as Blackburn was a small town every Black person seemed to know one another. My parents soon became friends with the Nelsons and it so happened they were both from Dominica. My parents were delighted to have another couple to socialise with and soon the two couples went out together at the weekend, to the Caribbean Club in Preston.

To a certain extent you are cocooned when you are at school, whilst out of school there were negative forces at play which impacted on our lives - one being the National Front.

Living in fear – The National Front Party

The National Front (NF) is a far-right British political party which was created in 1967 to oppose non-white immigration from the Commonwealth into the UK. The NF vote peaked in the 1976 local elections, when it won 19% of the vote in Leicester. Two short-lived populist phases of the NF during the 1970s saw the party try to appear more moderate, however under John Tyndall, who was the leader of the Party in 1972, the NF promoted white nationalism, fascism, had neo-Nazi sympathies and attracted violent subcultures (e.g., football hooligans and racist skinheads). Not only did we have the NF in Blackburn, on the political landscape we also had Enoch Powell, a Conservative member of Parliament, who in April 1968 gave a speech to a meeting of the Conservative Political Centre in Birmingham, England. His speech strongly criticised mass immigration, especially Commonwealth immigration to the United Kingdom, and the proposed Race Relations Bill. The Race Relations Act 1968 was an Act of the Parliament of the United Kingdom making it illegal to refuse housing, employment or public services to a person on the grounds of colour, race, ethnic or national origin in Great Britain. It also created the Community Relations Commission to promote "harmonious community relations". Enoch Powell's speech was famously named the "Rivers of Blood" speech; referring to mass immigration, he quoted a line from Virgil's Aeneid, an epic poem in twelve books that tells the story of the foundation of Rome from the Ashes of Troy. The quote says: *"As I look ahead, I* am filled with foreboding; like the Roman, I seem to see the River Tiber foaming with much blood."

The speech caused a political storm, making Powell one of the most talked about and divisive politicians in the country and it led to his controversial dismissal from the Shadow Cabinet by the Conservative party leader, Edward Heath. It was a frightening time for my family but particularly so for my sister and me. When the National Front was marching in Blackburn we had to stay inside our homes, hidden away. If we were out on the street whilst they were marching, we would be attacked. When I watch films about racism in America, where they depict Black people hiding from the Klu Klux Klan, a white supremacist, right-wing terrorist hate group, it reminds me of having to hide from the National Front. My husband experienced the same situation living in Preston, it was not safe for anyone of colour to be on the streets when they were marching.

Another impact was on football matches, where Black players were repeatedly racially abused. In an article by the UK Parliament from the House of Lords Library, for Black History Month: Racism in Football, published Wednesday, 27th October 2021, former players are asked to describe their experiences of racism in football. Brendon Baston from West Bromwich Albion says: "We'd get off the coach at away matches and the National Front would be right there in your face. In those days, we didn't have security and we'd have to run the gauntlet. We'd get to the players' entrance and there'd be spit on my jacket. It was a sign of the times. We coped. It wasn't a new phenomenon to us."

Similarly, being chased by skinheads and receiving verbal abuse in the street when I was a child was par for the course. I remember feeling anxious and physically shaking when I was informed that the National Front were marching, frightened that someone would tell them where we lived and that they would break into our home and brutalise us. When I was older, I was out late after visiting a friend and was walking home alone when a group of skinheads spotted me from afar, shouted at me and gave chase. I ran like my life depended on it (I was younger and fitter then)! At that time, the late 1970s, policemen still patrolled the streets and I managed to find a policeman and ask him to help me. He looked at me, a terrified young Black girl, and he was kind and sympathetic and ran them off!

Like most awful experiences, nothing is all bad, and racism during my formative years was overt rather than covert. However, Blackburn was a beautiful town, green and lush, and there was always a lot to do. We lived not too far from Queen's Park which was heaven for children, with play areas and a beautiful lake. In the summer holidays we would knock on people's doors near the park and ask for jam jars so we could collect frogspawn from the lake. Often, these complete strangers would offer us a cold drink and some cakes or biscuits; they were mainly older ladies who were very sweet to us. At weekends, my friends and I would go to Blue Bell Woods at Ribchester, where we would play for hours. We had a lot of freedom in those days, leaving home at 11am with money for lunch and returning home just in time for the evening meal. We were normally four girls, safety in numbers! I remember one day in particular when we decided to have an adventure and explore the countryside and we ended up climbing over a big gate that led to a farm. As we leapt off the other side of the gate we realised we were landing in mud, which was so deep it came to the top of our legs. The farmer arrived to help us out of the mud and we ended up sitting in his kitchen where his wife gave us hot chocolate and scones with home-made jam and cream. I must say, it tasted like nectar after all that time tramping around the countryside. Then he took us back to the main road so we could catch the bus home. I experienced a great deal of kindness like this and consequently was happy most of the time.

My Mum was an amazing woman, she arrived from Dominica to meet my father, a husband who she had not seen for six years, to a country where she had no friends or family. She was stoic, taking things in her stride and making a comfortable home for her family. She also found out about day trips to the seaside— we never knew where she was taking us, it was always a surprise. She would get up early and make sandwiches and off we would go. Our six-week summer holidays from school were an adventure and she made sure that we had a wonderful time. I remember visiting Blackpool, Morecombe, Clitheroe, and Southport. I have memories of halcyon days with Mum, sitting on the beach and building sandcastles, riding on the donkeys at Blackpool, going on endless rides on the funfair. Once I nearly fell off the merry-go-round, I was clinging on for dear life! We paddled in the sea, played ball, and ate burgers, chips, donuts, ice cream and candyfloss.

These happy memories mean that Blackpool has always been my go-to destination. It is a northwestern seaside resort on the Irish Sea coast of England, known for Blackpool Pleasure Beach, an amusement park. Built in 1894 the landmark Blackpool Tower houses a circus, a glass viewing platform and the Tower Ballroom, and Blackpool illuminations is an annual light show along the promenade. When I proclaim my love of Blackpool people look at me in astonishment and say, 'that tacky place'? Not only do I have memories from my childhood, but when Errol and I were first dating he lived in Leyland and I lived in Blackburn, so Blackpool was a convenient destination for both of us. We would spend hours walking down the promenade or sitting on the beach. In later years, we would take our children there, particularly when they were younger, because sitting on the beach with a ball kept them busy and happy for hours. That was until at five years old our daughter was able to read. She looked down the promenade and said "What's that over there? It says fun house, can we have fun and go in there?" That was the end of our cheap days out in Blackpool! Summer holidays for my children always included a trip to Blackpool and I have taken the grandchildren to Madam Tussauds and Blackpool Zoo, they just love it!

CHAPTER 3
Maintaining our Caribbean culture

At home both my parents spoke patois, or Creole (Kwéyòl), but we were not permitted to speak it. At the time it was seen as detrimental to your future success if you didn't speak English well and as our parents' desire was for all their children to be successful in life, speaking Creole was not seen as a prerequisite. However, the table has turned and now it is part of Dominican culture to speak Creole, some of the radio programmes are spoken in Creole only, and I wish I had learnt to speak my native language as a girl.

Apart from the language my parents were very proud of their Dominican culture, particularly our food and the way in which it was cooked. We ate tasty broths, seasoned chicken and rice, red beans, and lots of steamed fish. My mother was ahead of her time when it came to food and nutrition, and we were only allowed to have chips or a Chinese takeaway once a week. Every morning she gave us a spoonful of cod liver oil, which was vile. Once a month we had a "purge", which involved giving us all Senna Pods. These needed to be steeped in water and were then made into a tea. Unfortunately my mum did not calculate the fact that we had only one lavatory and gave us all the Senna tea at the same time. You can imagine the chaos that ensued, with all four girls fighting for the loo! Our normal eating habits involved plenty of vegetables, protein and, when she could get them from the Caribbean grocery, yams, sweet potatoes and callaloo, which is like spinach. At weekends only we would have the divinely delicious carrot juice, or Guinness punch, which were sweetened with condensed milk and spiced with cinnamon and nutmeg. There was a man called Oliver who used to come to our house to deliver fish once a week. Mum would cook red snapper in a delicious sauce with seasoned red kidney beans.

Every Christmas Mum would always buy a huge turkey which was so big that Dad had difficulty getting it into the oven. It was well seasoned with garlic, herbs, and other spices. Mum would leave it to marinade all night and get up at 6am to put it in the oven. Christmas Day always started with the gorgeous smell of roasting turkey in our house, and because it was so large we'd be eating turkey for days afterwards. I remember Mum's turkey, mayonnaise, and stuffing sandwiches— if I close my eyes, I can still taste them. My daughter had planned to sit with my mum and write a book about all her recipes, such was her cooking prowess, but sadly Mum died before this could happen. However, I feel that my good skin and good overall health is down to Mum setting the right foundations for us when we were young.

Social interaction

My parents naturally tended to gravitate towards other Dominicans because they had a shared life experience. There were two families with whom we had regular social interaction: the Wiltshires, Uncle Phansoe and Aunty Clarina, who were friends of my parents from Dominica and who were also related by family; and Maureen and James Nelson. At weekends we would visit one another's houses, the children would play together, and we would eat Caribbean food. These gatherings were fun, and I have lots of happy memories of those visits.

Preston was the town we went to for entertainment and there were two particular clubs where Caribbean people would go to for an evening out: The Jalgos Sports and Social Club, which was founded in 1962 and at the time was mostly frequented by Jamaicans; and the Caribbean Club, which was frequented by the smaller island immigrants, such as Dominicans, people from St. Kitts, St Lucia, etc. These two clubs formed the hub of my parents' social activity where they could meet friends, have a drink and dance to calypso and soca music. At the time a Trinidadian calypso vocalist, songwriter and guitarist called Mighty Sparrow was very popular, known as the "Calypso King of the World"! As children we heard his music so often that we knew all the words to his songs.

My parents would also have parties at home. We children would normally have to go to bed when the party was in full swing but quite often my father would have us entertain their guests, under the disapproving eye of my mother. He would put some music on and we would dance to entertain the crowd. If we weren't getting the moves right, Dad would say "Come on girls, a bit more shoulder" or "a bit more footwork". I loved it because I am not a shy person and would love the adulation, which the adults would find highly amusing and there would be thunderous applause, whereas my sister Liza was shy and for her it was a bit of an ordeal.

I come from a warm and loving home, where there was a lot of fun and laughter. On winter days, when we were bored, my father would disappear and then make an entrance wearing Mum's very large afro wig, complete with his moustache, roll his trousers up so that we could see his legs and prance around to amuse us. He had the most fabulous legs and Mum was always envious of them. He was a great entertainer, and we would often laugh until we cried. There was always music playing in our house but on Sundays, as in most Caribbean households, the only music we were allowed to play was Gospel music, it was considered sacrilegious to play anything else. My Mum's favourite artist was Jim Reeves who, although better known for his country and western music, also sang some powerful gospel music. Whenever I hear his distinctive smooth, warm baritone, I immediately think of my mother.

Apart from the food Christmas was a time for celebration in our house, the Christmas tree twinkling merrily with lots of gifts beneath it, playing games, or sitting around the television watching films. Often my father's workmates would call round for a drink and a piece of cake. Both my parents were kind and compassionate people, and we would often have strangers staying at our house. One night Dad brought home a couple from Ireland who had nowhere to stay for the night. Mum got out of bed, we girls were all put into one room, and she put fresh sheets on the bed for them. They were made welcome and stayed with us for a few days. That was typical of my parents, if someone needed help they would not hesitate to offer food, room, and board. At both their funerals people spoke about times when my parents had helped them without expecting anything in return. My mum was the kind of woman whose first words were, when you walked into the house and before your bottom could touch the chair, "What can I offer you, coffee, tea or a soft drink?" That is the way we were brought up and my sisters and I are exactly the same, we like to be very hospitable to our guests.

Religion

The most common religion in Dominica is Christianity, with most practitioners identifying as Roman Catholic. My father was not a religious person, but my mother was. All four girls were christened in church and we were brought up as Roman Catholics but my parents quickly became disillusioned when they arrived in the UK. They attended a nearby church where they received a lot of stares and were made to feel uncomfortable. After the Mass, the priest approached my parents as they were leaving and told them thank you for coming but please don't come back next week! This galvanised my mum into looking for a church that would welcome us. At one point we attended a different church every week, from Pentecostal to Baptist, Methodist etc. We travelled all over Lancashire in my mum's quest for a welcoming congregation.

During my childhood, I found aspects of the Catholic church a little confusing, specifically confession. Whilst attending primary school we had to go to confession, and I remember having to invent sins to confess to. My life was spent playing with my friends and reading books, so I wasn't sure how I had sinned and struggled to say anything in the confessional. The nuns also threatened us with being held in Purgatory, a place of purification or punishment where, according to Roman Catholic belief, the souls of those who die in a state of grace are made ready for heaven. I found this terrifying as a child and had nightmares about it. As we grew older, we were allowed to make our own decisions as to whether we wanted to attend church or not and my older sister and I withdrew from attending Mass.

Mum continued searching for a church where she felt comfortable and could worship in the way she wanted to. The Catholic church was stiff and formal with many rituals and her early experience of being rejected when she first arrived in the UK coloured her judgment. The Pentecostal church was a little bit too much for Mum. It is a very physical environment where people are very vocal and interactive, whereas Mum was a little reserved and just wanted to pray quietly. That's not to say that all Pentecostal churches are like that, but the ones we visited required a lot of participation. We were used to the Catholic church: stand; sing; kneel down; stand up; sit; and pray quietly. However, on 31 May 1982, when Pope John Paul II visited Manchester, Mum insisted that Errol and I take her to Heaton Park where we joined the crowd of 250,000 people to hear him celebrate Mass. Mum was thrilled but Errol found it a bit tiresome, as he was the one driving through the large crowds of people and it was a little chaotic. He was doing it for my mum as he had no desire to see the Pope.

When Mum returned to Dominica in 1984 she finally found what she was looking for, a church in her community where she was welcomed, respected, and loved. Also, as an older member of the church she became a church elder, providing support to others, a role she relished.

CHAPTER 4
Creating a new life

Moving on up!

The Collaire family moved from a small, terraced house, to a beautiful semi-detached house in a cul-de-sac, not too far from our secondary school in the Shadsworth area of Blackburn. It was a lovely house, Mum and Dad were both proud because this was evidence that they were doing well. Mum was a housewife and worked part-time and Dad worked full-time on nights. He was a vulcanizer, someone who vulcanizes rubber to improve its strength and resiliency. He worked on a piecework basis which meant that he was paid a fixed rate for each unit produced or action performed, regardless of time. His job was making slippers which had rubber soles and I remember being taken for a tour of the factory where Dad showed us what he did. He was good at his job because he constantly surpassed the number of slippers made on his shift. There was no ceiling on the amount of money you could earn once the 'piece' was fully completed and it passed the quality standard. It was through Dad's hard work and Mum's financial savvy that the family amassed sufficient savings to purchase a larger house in Blackburn. And of course, the other benefit of Dad's job was that we always had more than one pair of beautiful, warm slippers!

For the love of books

As an adolescent I discovered a love of books and although I enjoyed listening to music, socialising, and visiting the countryside, my most enduring hobby is reading. Every time I received my pocket money, I would run to the bookstore and buy a book. I began with the Mills & Boon romances, alongside Anne of Green Gables and Pippy Longstocking and moved on to Georgette Heyer. At school we studied more classical literature and I loved books by Jane Austen, Thomas Hardy, George Eliot and the Brontës; Wuthering Heights was given to us as the book to read for our English Literature exam. I was a voracious reader and if my mum couldn't find me she knew that I would be curled up reading somewhere. Books opened up an interesting world to me where I would genuinely lose myself. Every time a book ended I felt a sense of loss because I was leaving the characters behind.

Growing up, my taste in books became more varied and I fell in love with Agatha Christie, purchased all her books and even now I am not averse to reading them again and again. My interest in authors created a thirst for knowledge about their lives and I have visited Howarth in Yorkshire where the Brontës lived; it was fascinating! They have dresses on display that were worn by the Bronte sisters, I marvel at how small they were. Looking at the size of their clothes as grown women, I can see why a lot of women in those days died young. They needed a good, healthy, well-balanced meal! I have also visited Hill Top Farm, where Beatrix Potter wrote thirteen of her twenty-three books, as well as Agatha Christie's home in Devon.

I developed an interest in American authors after seeing the programme *Roots* on television and read the book, by Alex Haley, which developed my interest in books such as *The Color Purple* by Alice Walker and *I Know Why the Caged Bird Sings* by Maya Angelou. I also enjoy the novels and films of Terry McMillan, in particular *How Stella Got her Groove Back* and *Waiting to Exhale*. Most recently I have enjoyed reading Michelle Obama's book *Belonging*.

As I developed my career in Human Resource Management, I added textbooks and journals to my reading material, including books on management development, organisational development, strategic thinking, learning and development, coaching and mentoring. I consider reading these books to be part of my job, it is important to keep abreast of what is happening in your profession. But for recreation and fun I read a variety of genres. If something is bothering me, or if I have a question about an issue, I search online and find an appropriate book to read. At various times in my life, when I have felt troubled or challenged, I found a book that answered my question, or provoked a different way of looking at the problem. My bookshelves reveal who I really am as a person. In our house in the UK I had full bookshelves in every room, and I am happy to say that they have now found a new home in our house in Dominica.

Currently my Kindle is my device of choice for reading. I still buy textbooks, but for my everyday reading I love Kindle Unlimited which allows me to read many books as part of my Amazon membership. Most weeks, I receive a notification telling me that I have read every day for the past month or so. Reading is a pleasure for me. My ideal day is a rainy day and I am inside the house, sitting next to a window so I can see outside, with a book in my hand and a warm drink—total and complete bliss.

Love of the Lake District

I mentioned earlier that I received pocket money as a child, a generous sum of £5 per week to spend as I wanted. We had to purchase all our feminine requirements from this sum, however, we were still left with a substantial amount to have fun with. I spent mine mainly on books and saved the rest. Mum knew about my saving habit and if she ran out of money before pay day, she would always ask me for a loan. Apart from buying books, I saved for any school trips I wanted to attend. These were mainly visiting various parts of the countryside and included walking and cycling holidays. As I grew up, I developed a love for the countryside and went on school trips to the Lake District National Park. I spent many happy holidays in Ambleside, Coniston, Hawkshead, to name but a few of the lovely towns and villages. On one of these trips, we were taken to the local cinema to see the film *The Sound of Music* with Julie Andrews and on the way back to our cabins we walked up the hill singing "The hills are alive, with the sound of music"! I loved it! As an adult, I have retained my love of the Lake District and have been back frequently with friends. One of our favourite locations is Wastwater where, along with five girlfriends, I climbed the Great Gable, a mountain with an elevation of 2,949 ft (nearly 900 m), and one of the most popular of the Lakeland fells.

I loved walking around the countryside with a group of people, admiring the beauty and having conversations. As a child I had planned to live in the Lake District when I grew up. Sadly, that didn't happen but I have been a regular visitor all my life, until I moved to the Caribbean. The author Alfred Wainwright published seven volumes that make up his *Pictorial Guide to the Lakeland Fells*, detailing the 214 principal hills and mountains of the Lake District. This was shown as a television series called *Wainwright Walks* which I watched in fascination, pointing out places that I had already visited and earmarking the places I wanted to go.

Errol and I have a mutual love of the countryside and visiting well known beauty spots, and when the children came along we shared this love with them. Weekends would be spent visiting Glossop in the Peak District, taking long walks. In the summer we'd drive around Scotland or go to the Eden Project in Cornwall, a former clay mine with no soil or plants which has been transformed into a beautiful global garden. As you walk through the huge Biomes you can experience the world's largest rainforest or the calm fragrance of the Mediterranean. There are extensive outdoor gardens too, and artworks to explore, it is an immersive experience. The last time Errol and I visited they were growing banana plants and other tropical fruit that we have in the Caribbean. But of all the places that I have visited in the UK, the Lake District has the number one spot in my heart, with Scotland coming a close second.

For the love of baking

As I mentioned earlier in this book, I have three sisters. Each of us had a different skill. My older sister Liza was great with hair from an early age. As the eldest, she had the job of plaiting our hair and on Sunday afternoons, we'd sit on a chair whilst she styled our hair for school the following week. I used to annoy her because after she'd spent hours creating a wonderful style for me, I would pick at my hair whilst playing or watching TV. I still have this habit, which my husband finds equally annoying! My own skill was baking. At weekends I would bake cakes, scones, jam tarts, pies, and pastries for the whole family. I loved baking and still do, however, I knew that I wouldn't make a career of it because I only like baking when I feel like it, I wouldn't enjoy it if I had to bake every day. My sister Susan was the family seamstress, sewing, mending and creating her own clothes. My youngest sister, Sharon, has the biggest and kindest heart. She was known as the family nurse and if you were ill she would look after you. When my father was dying of cancer, at home in Dominica, Sharon helped my mum a lot with his care during his final days.

As adults, my sister Liza pursued a career in hairdressing, gaining her qualifications and becoming one of the most sought-after hairdressers in Manchester and then London. She moved back to the Caribbean to look after our mother after our father died and created a name for herself as a brilliant hairdresser in Dominica. Liza and Sharon now live in the family home in Dominica, Liza still enjoys hairdressing but only for a few select clients and she also owns a shop that Sharon helps her with. Liza has worked for the government, training fledgling hairdressers and helping them to become young entrepreneurs, passing on her expertise to others. Susan became a seamstress and makes bespoke fashion items, she still lives in the UK and is planning to join us one day in Dominica. Sharon did not become a nurse, she emigrated with our parents when they returned to Dominica and remained there, helping with the bakery before becoming a mother herself.

CHAPTER 5
Time to grow up!

Making sense of the world

Just as I was taking my 'O' Levels, as they were called then, my parents made an attempt to return to Dominica. On this occasion my mother left with my younger sisters, Susan and Sharon, and my father remained in the UK to keep earning an income to send to Mum so she could establish a home for them. My sister Liza had already left home and was living in a rented apartment, so it was just me and my father. I was nearly seventeen and wanted to have some freedom and go out with my friends but my father disagreed; he wanted me to concentrate on my studies. My father and I are both very volatile and so we had a difference of opinion and I left to go and live with Liza. I took my exams as planned and managed to pass six 'O' Levels even without my books, which I'd left at home. My mum was upset that I had left home and insisted that if she had been there I would never have left, which was true.

I started my first job as a clerk typist for Keith Newmark Limited in Blackburn, which sold plastic planters, and began to understand the world of work and organisational culture. It was a female office with the only males being the owner of the business and his son. It was my first job and as I was learning I made mistakes, my attention to detail was not as good as it should have been. The supervisor, Danutia, was very patient with me and kept coaching and mentoring me until my performance improved. I enjoyed working there and was made to feel part of the team.

However, the salary of an office junior was not high, and unlike most office juniors I had rent to pay and food to buy. Liza and I also worked in the evenings as waitresses at a hotel, which augmented our income and allowed us to buy new shoes and clothes to go dancing at weekends.

I wasn't sure what I wanted to do, career-wise, so my sister advised getting a qualification in business studies which would give me a good grounding for most things. I was definitely *not* in my prime at this time of my life! My days were spent working either my day job or waitressing in the evenings. At weekends, when we were not working, we would go to the disco, as both Liza and I loved to dance. We would arrive and purchase a large glass of juice with lots of ice, place it on a table near the dancefloor and I would keep it in my line of sight. If I wasn't able to see my drink because of the number of people on the dance floor, I would throw it away. At the time there was a saying about someone "slipping you a Mickey Finn", which was slang for someone surreptitiously putting drugs in your drink, rendering the unsuspecting drinker helpless. My friends had shared harrowing stories with me, of waking up next to a complete stranger, with no memory of what happened the night before. This was one of my biggest fears and consequently I guarded my drink diligently. We would spend all night on the dance floor and keep topping up our fruit juice. It was the jazz funk era and we were huge fans. We spent many an evening in Romeo and Juliette's in Blackburn, Angel's in Burnley, and Clouds in Preston.

I didn't limit myself to only jazz funk music, it was the late 1970s early 80s, my disco days. We used to watch *Top of the Pops*, the British pop music programme that was shown every Thursday evening on BBC television. Artists and groups with hit records performed live on the programme, or we saw their latest videos. Every week *Pan's People*, a group of scantily clad, attractive women would dance suggestively to one of the hits. When I lived at home, I remember my father lifting his eyes from the paper he was reading when Pan's People made an appearance. I enjoyed it all — the Bee Gees, Tom Jones, Barry White, Diana Ross, Motown— the list is endless and I loved dancing the night away! There was a strange phenomenon at this time; if the artist had a sexy voice, like Barry White, the women in the audience used to throw their underwear on stage whilst he was singing! I always thought it was a very strange thing to do, albeit it was considered a way of showing appreciation for the artist. I remember a reporter asking Barry White how he felt about being the object of desire by so many women, hence the knicker throwing, and he said he didn't like it and he wished they'd stop!

I was not in my prime regarding my life experience or my corporate competence, but I was in my prime when it came to my physical peak, or so I thought. My sister and I didn't do a weekly shop to buy food, we considered this a waste of money. Most days our meals consisted of instant soup in a cup or a sandwich. At weekends we would treat ourselves to a packet of digestive biscuits with a cup of tea. Our focus was on having a great body. I was at my most desired and ideal weight of 9st (about 57kg), according to the Body Mass Index (BMI), which is a person's weight in kilograms or pounds, divided by the square of height in meters or feet. A high BMI can indicate high body fatness. It was important to remain slim so that I could fit into my bohemian harem pants, which were the height of fashion at that time, together with winkle picker shoes and a boob tube! I was ready to hit the dancefloor!

The Rules of dating according to my mum

My mother was the most amazing woman, her thought processes were way beyond her time. As soon I was old enough to start dating boys my mum gave me the following advice, which I followed to the letter:

When you go out on a date take enough money with you to get a taxi home. If your date behaves inappropriately, you have sufficient funds to get home on your own.

Never sleep with a boyfriend on the first date, take time to get to know him, meet his family and friends and find out his true personality. If he doesn't want to wait until you are ready, say goodbye, because you are worth waiting for.

If someone you don't know offers to buy you a drink, always go to the bar with them to ensure that there is only your drink in that glass, and nothing else!

If you leave your drink unattended, never go back to it and certainly don't drink it!

If you are offered a tablet for a headache etc., do not swallow it unless you see the packet it was taken from as evidence that it actually is an aspirin or paracetamol.

Do not take drugs of any kind unless prescribed by your doctor.

Never get in a car with more than one man that you don't know. You may have a chance to fight back with one, but with two it would be impossible.

There are many perils out there for young people living on their own. Mum's advice was timely and I think it kept me safe. Reading my story of trying to navigate adulthood and avoid any nasty pitfalls demonstrates that at nineteen years old, I was definitely not in my prime, I was learning how to navigate life, behave as an adult, and support myself.

Meeting my husband

One Friday evening I had gone to bed early, planning to read a good book, when my friend, Suzanna Nelson, called round. She said she was going to the Caribbean Club in Preston, her mum was waiting outside in the car, and would I like to go with them? I said no at first, but she said I was being boring so I got myself ready and jumped in the car. When we arrived, I was glad that I had decided to go and we were soon on the dance floor, strutting our funky stuff! Then a rather shy young man approached us and asked Suzanna if she wanted to dance. We ended up all dancing together and afterwards we sat down and he joined us. At first he was chatting to Suzanna, who wasn't really engaging in conversation with him, and then he and I started talking. We spoke for quite a while and it ended with him asking for my telephone number. I didn't have a telephone at home, so I took his number. This young man was called Errol Strachan. It was October 1980, I had just turned nineteen and he was twenty-four years old.

Strangely enough, the following day was a Saturday and my sister and I, together with a friend of hers, had arranged to go and see a fortune teller. We were young girls at the beginning of our lives, and wanted to know about our future prospects. The person we went to see was famous in the area, her name was Old Mother Redcap, and she did indeed wear a little red hat! She lived in a cottage and looked homely. We each had a private consultation with her. When it was my turn, she had me shuffle a pack of cards and lay some on the table, and then read my fortune. Her exact words to me were "The man you met last night you are going to marry; you will have a girl and then a boy and you will return to the Caribbean to live." I looked at her in complete astonishment, not believing a word of what she said. I had only just met Errol and really didn't know him very well. Not only that, but I was also happy with my life in the UK and had no intention of returning to the Caribbean! I paid her the £5 fee, which was what was expected, but I just thought it was all pie in the sky, firmly believing that she mentioned the possibility of me living in the Caribbean because I was Black. I put it all behind me and never thought of it again.

The following Monday morning I went to work and was chatting with my colleagues about our weekend adventures. I shared the whole story with them, ending with the fact that because we were so different in personalities, I was not sure that Errol and I would meet again. He was very quiet in contrast to my outgoing, gregarious personality. They urged me to give Errol a ring and insisted that as the boss was out, I could go and ring him privately from his office. I had the piece of paper with his name and number on, and so I rang and introduced myself because I wasn't sure if he would remember me. He did, and we arranged to go on a date that weekend to a nightclub called Kitterman's in Oldham. That was in 1980 and in June 2022 we celebrated our fortieth wedding anniversary!

Naturally, we've had many challenges along the way, the biggest of which was meeting Errol's mum for the first time. We had gone out to a night club for the evening and as it was the 1980's I was dressed in a fashionable boob tube, fishnet stockings and a mini skirt, the perfect outfit for going dancing. Halfway through the evening Errol announced that he would like to take me to meet his mother; I was still living in Blackburn but we were having an evening out in Preston, which was where Errol's family lived. I looked at my outfit in alarm, thinking "This isn't the kind of outfit one wears for meeting someone's mother!" I knew that Errol's mother was a church going, God fearing woman and I just had a feeling that she would not approve of me. However, after a few futile protests I gave in, and we drove to his parents' home.

Thankfully, it was winter and I was wearing a long coat, so I fastened it up from right under my chin down to my ankles, so that none of my disco clothes were visible. However, when I entered the room there was a fire burning and the heat was intense, and it wasn't long before beads of sweat started to trickle down my face. Errol's mother kept offering to take my coat, but I steadfastly refused, insisting that I was just fine. From our initial meeting I got the impression that his mother didn't take to me at all. I am a reflection of my family; outgoing, talkative, laughing at every opportunity. Errol's family are more reflective and sometimes I found the silence in his parents' home a little unnerving, just as he found the noise in my family home overwhelming. In our forty years of marriage his mother never warmed to me. I was not a church girl, I was not Jamaican, and I was far too noisy. When my parents first met Errol, my mum asked me in the kitchen, "Does he speak?" My father kept trying to get him to go to the pub for a drink, but Errol isn't a drinker, so although he would occasionally go along to the pub with Dad he would, more often than not, try to get out of it. Errol's parents' opinion of me never changed over the years but my parents grew to love him, in fact my father was so fond of him that he made him an Executor of his Will.

As I mentioned earlier, Errol did not come to the UK until he was sixteen years old. His parents both worked, but it was his mother who was best known in Preston and beyond. She ran her own events planning and bridal business, where she would organise a whole wedding from dressing the venue to making the bride's dress, the cake etc. It was difficult for Errol to adjust to his new life in England and soon after emigrating to the UK he joined the Queen's Lancashire Regiment. He spent two years in the British Army and spent a lot of time in Cyprus, where he learned to ski on the Troodos Mountains.

Errol always had a yearning to return to Jamaica and within two years of arriving in the UK he saved his wages so that he could return to Jamaica on holiday to visit his friends and family. As I grew to know Errol more I realised that he was very ambitious and even in his twenties he had plans for his future. I remember visiting his apartment in Leyland, Lancashire. It was beautifully and tastefully decorated and I could see that a lot of thought had gone into creating a lovely home for himself. At weekends Errol took flying lessons, as he wanted to fly is own plane one day, and I would often watch him playing squash at the club he was a member of. He continued to play squash for many years but married life and two children meant there was no money for expensive hobbies such as learning to fly.

Shortly after Errol and I met, my sister Liza and I decided to move from our flat in Blackburn to Manchester, where there were more opportunities for work. We had lived in Blackburn since we were six and eight respectively and felt the draw of the big city! I wasn't quite sure if my relationship with Errol was serious or not, but we kept in touch and met mainly at weekends. As fate would have it, Errol was in the process of making a career change and wanted to study to be an engineer. The course he was interested in was at Salford University, in Greater Manchester. Liza and I lived in Salford and later moved to Longsight, an inner-city area of Manchester three miles south of the city centre, so it was a big step when Errol and I decided to move into our own little flat together. However, Liza and I still saw each other almost every day and Errol used to comment that, although we had only seen each other the previous day, we would still chat for hours as soon as we got together.

We were young and not earning a lot of money, and Errol had kept his flat on in Leyland so our flat in Longsight was not our main home. In fact it was a basic bedsit, one room containing everything. I was discussing those early days with

Errol and he reminded me that everything was on a meter. The lights were on a meter, as was the oven. To have a shower you had to put ten pence in the slot and on more than one occasion I'd be standing there fully lathered up with soap and the water would run out. If you didn't have another ten pence handy you were in trouble! It was also infested with mice and often, as we were trying to sleep on our single bed, we would hear the patter of tiny feet on the linoleum. At first I was terrified of the mice, but then I got used to it and kept a shoe handy to throw at them. We loved weekends when we could go to Errol's flat in Leyland and bask in the beauty of the gorgeous English countryside, as well as the luxury of a hot bath and all the wonderful amenities.

I remember one particularly awful Christmas in the "bedsit from hell". The weather forecast predicted temperatures dropping to -1°C or below, with lots of snow, and we were stuck in the bedsit over Christmas. We ventured out to Longsight market to purchase some food. A turkey was out of our price range but we saw a small chicken at the meat market and we bought some carrots and sprouts to go with it. We didn't possess a fridge so we had to be creative in order to keep the chicken from decomposing before we could cook and eat it. There was a skylight window in the ceiling, so we tied a piece of string around the chicken's ankle and threw it onto the roof until we were ready. What we didn't count on was the temperature dropping to -6°C that night, and in the morning the chicken was frozen solid! That experience still makes us laugh when we stop to look back on our life together.

CHAPTER 6
Becoming a wife and mother

Errol and I were married at Carey Baptist Church in Preston in June 1982. The church is still there, recorded in the National Heritage List for England as a designated Grade II Listed Building. It was a beautiful ceremony. My father gave me away and my three sisters, Liza, Susan and Sharon, were bridesmaids, as well as my husband's sister, Paulette. We had the usual last-minute panics, such as my dress being completed at the last minute; delayed fittings; bridesmaids' dresses being flattering for some and not others, but the most stressful issue was our photographer. We had booked her in good time, a year before the date of the wedding, and we had a signed contract. However, nearer to the time, she received a better offer, a larger wedding that would bring her more income, and she contacted us and tried to extricate herself from the contract. We were having none of it and insisted that she honour the terms of the contract, mainly because it was impossible to secure another photographer at such short notice.

On our wedding day she arrived late, took only the essential photos, and left so she could go on to her big, important wedding. I do have a wedding album, however, the intimate photographs capturing our guests, showing the atmosphere and the little quirks that happen at a wedding, are not there. It was 1982, the mobile phone had not yet been invented, and we had to rely on a good photographer, so I was very disappointed. I am sure every bride has a story to tell about their wedding day. On a more positive note, after the wedding we had our luncheon at the Tickled Trout Hotel, Preston. It is a lovely venue, where our guests could look out at the stunning views of the river Ribble whilst enjoying their repast. It was a beautiful wedding, no bride could have asked for more. I remember sitting at the top table in my lace dress, made by my mother-in-law, looking around at our friends and family gathered together as the toast was made, my mum and dad looking on with pride. It was a memorable moment of pure happiness for me.

According to Old Mother Redcap, the fortune teller, I would marry Errol and then have two children, a girl and then a boy. I should have taken more notice!

PRIME

My daughter Rhia was born just a week after my twenty-first birthday, in October 1982, and my son Ricky was born in April 1984. I would have liked four children, but my husband felt that we were lucky enough to have a girl and a boy, and in order to give them the best that we could in life two children were sufficient. My children were my parents' first grandchildren and they adored them. They still lived in Blackburn, twenty-six miles from Manchester, and I visited them most weekends. Sometimes I would go alone with the children; I loved spending time with my mum and dad and would go there as often as I could. They were also happy to babysit if Errol and I wanted to go out. We did not have a large family in Blackburn, it was just my parents and the four girls, however, my parents did have relatives in Preston, Mr Phansoe Wiltshire and his wife Clarina. They had five children and we had some great playmates. There would be visits to Preston, when Mum and Dad would chat in patois, there would be good food, lots of laughter, a big family get-together.

A marriage is two families merging together. Errol was part of a large extended family and because the main part of his childhood was spent in Jamaica we visited the island as much as possible. Each time we visited, Errol would hire a car and off we would go sightseeing. Over the years, I have been to the Blue Mountains and tasted the world-renowned coffee, the Blue Lagoon, Negril beach, Rose Hall, Devon House for their famous ice-cream, and we have visited the Kingston Museum and Emancipation Park. During our visits to Jamaica I met and became friends with Errol's aunts and uncles. He was particularly close to his Aunty Rosa and Uncle Tony who eventually moved to America, as did many of Errol's relatives. The bond between Errol and Rosa is a strong one and we frequently visited her and Tony in Miami, and she would reciprocate and visit us in Manchester. Rosa took us under her wing, regaling me with stories of Errol as a young child, much to his chagrin. The children loved visiting their Aunty Rosa and on one occasion she organised a trip to Disney World for our family, which we really appreciated. She was an excellent host, each time we visited she would plan a trip for us, it was always a rollercoaster ride of fun.

A big milestone in my life was when my mum immigrated back to Dominica for the final time. She went ahead of my father to establish a home and get things ready, whilst Dad remained in the UK and kept working to send money that was needed to fund a new life for them, and for my youngest sister Sharon, who was to go with them. I was extremely close to my mum and begged her not go; my daughter Rhia was three at the time, and Ricky was just eighteen months old. Before my mum left, we had a long conversation wherein I asked her again not to go. She explained to me that she longed to live in the land of her birth. The English weather didn't suit her, she wasn't happy, and she couldn't remain in the country purely for my sake. At the time I thought she was selfish but I was young, still in my twenties, and didn't understand that my mum was not only my mother but a woman in her own right, with hopes and dreams of her own. Now in my sixties myself I understand what she was trying to tell me, and of course history has repeated itself— I have left my children and grandchildren in the UK and returned to live in Dominica, the land of my birth.

My father remained in the UK for another two years and he was a fabulous grandfather. He would come and visit us regularly, always bringing something for the children, playing with them endlessly, teaching them how to ride their bikes and allowing them to climb all over him. The children loved him, and he loved them. I felt devastated when he finally left England to join my mother and sister in Dominica. I missed them so much and felt that there was a big hole in my life. My sisters were living their own lives, Liza had moved to London and Susan was living in Birmingham. Although I was still relatively young, I realised that I had to start creating my own little family, just as my mother was the lynchpin of our family. I put my energy and focus into building a home for my husband, myself, and our children. Both Errol and I were focused on giving our two children the best life possible. That meant securing their future in the land of their birth. I mentioned earlier that I came to the UK as part of the Windrush generation. We came from the Commonwealth, believing that we had a home in the UK, which is why the Windrush scandal was so shocking.

Future-proofing our life - the Windrush scandal

Both Errol and I thought it was important to keep up with the international and national news. We also attended events at the West Indian Centre, at Westwood Street in Manchester. These meetings were important, not only to keep up to date with what was happening in the Caribbean, but also with valuable information regarding the Caribbean population in the UK. During the late 1980's we started hearing news about a potential future threat to all Caribbean migrants who lived in the UK but who did not possess British Citizenship or hold British passports. The rumour was that in the future this would mean that you would not be able to access the National Health Service, or work in the UK. Errol and I were planning to build our life in the UK and we wanted to protect our children's future so we both applied for British Citizenship and became British passport holders. This decision was a wise one, not least because both Errol and I were to become international consultants working in over twenty-five countries around the world and our British passports were beneficial.

Quite a few of our fellow countrymen refused to take the same steps because they were convinced that we were safe, as members of the Commonwealth family. They felt that by giving up the passport from their country of birth, they were rejecting their roots. Sadly, the rumours were correct and the Windrush scandal has had a catastrophic impact on many Caribbean migrants who made their homes in the UK.

The Windrush generation is described as people arriving in the UK between 1948 and 1971. The HMT Empire Windrush was one of the first ships which docked in Tilbury, on 22 June 1948, bringing workers from Jamaica, Trinidad & Tobago and other islands to help fill post-war UK labour shortages. The British

Nationality Act 1948 gave citizens of the United Kingdom and Colonies status, and the right of settlement in the UK to everyone who was at that time a British subject by virtue of having been born in a British colony. Between 1948 and 1970, nearly half a million people moved from the Caribbean to Britain. Working age adults and children travelled from the Caribbean to join parents or grandparents in the UK and many children travelled without their own passports. My father travelled to the UK in 1961 and I followed in 1967, and my family are all classed as being part of the Windrush generation.

Having a legal right to come to the UK, they neither needed nor were given any documents upon entry to the UK, nor following changes in immigration laws in the early 1970s. Many worked or attended schools in the UK without any official documentary record of their having done so, other than the same records as any UK-born citizen.

A BBC article, (*BBC News, Windrush Generation: Who are they and why are they facing problems? 16th April 2018 updated 24th November 2021*) first published when the Windrush Scandal broke in 2018, was updated in November 2021 when the UK government apologised for deportations and threats made to Commonwealth citizens' children. Despite living and working in the UK for decades, many were told they were there illegally because of a lack of official paperwork. The Home Office had kept no record of those granted leave to remain and had issued no paperwork, making it difficult for Windrush arrivals to prove their legal status. In 2010 the British Government destroyed landing cards belonging to Windrush migrants who believed that because they came from British colonies that were not independent, they were British citizens. Those who lacked documents were told they needed evidence in order to continue working, qualify for NHS treatment, or even remain in the UK. Changes to immigration law by successive governments left people fearful about their status.

A review of historical cases found that at least eighty-three individuals who had arrived before 1973 had been removed from the country. In April 2018, then Prime Minister Theresa May apologised and an inquiry was announced, and subsequently a compensation scheme established. However, the Home Affairs Committee – a cross party body of MP's which examines immigration and security, said that by the end of September 2021 only a fifth of these had come forward, and only a quarter had received compensation. More than twenty individuals died before receiving any money.

In June 2020, the BBC broadcast a feature-length factual television drama called *Sitting in Limbo,* about the real-life experiences of a Jamaican born British man, Anthony Bryan, one of the victims of the UK Home Office's hostile environment policy on immigration. Bryan had lived in the UK for fifty years when his life was turned upside down because the Home Office mistakenly classified him as an illegal migrant. My husband and I watched this film in complete silence, the pain and horror written on our faces. It was heart wrenching to watch a decent, honest, hardworking man losing his home and everything he owned, then being thrown into a detention centre. He came out of the experience looking completely traumatised. We both said, "There but for the grace of God go I", because we knew it could have so easily have been us.

Windrush Day

The good news is that there is now a day in the United Kingdom called Windrush Day, which is observed annually on 22 June although it is not officially a Bank Holiday. It was introduced in June 2018 on the 70th anniversary of the Windrush migration and was instituted following a successful campaign led by Patrick Vernon OBE, a political activist of Jamaican heritage and former Labour councillor in the London Borough of Hackney. He is a filmmaker and cultural historian and runs his own social enterprise promoting the history of diverse communities.

At the time of writing this book we are celebrating the 75th Anniversary of Windrush Day. Over the years the contribution made to British society by Black people has never been recognised and, for me, this celebration warms my heart. Although Caribbean migrants arrived by invitation and to help rebuild Britain, on arrival they were met with racism and lack of acknowledgment of their professional skills and had to live in very different living conditions.

Having lived all my life with the negative portrayal of Black people, from an historical viewpoint we have very few documentaries about Black scholars, mathematicians, or scientists, and from the media we have seen biased reporting of Black events. For example, the Notting Hill Carnival in London is one of the biggest carnivals in Europe and it has been established since 1959. It attracts over a million people and is world famous, encompassing our history and culture. However, if you watch the news, wanting to hear about this amazing event, it is always a very short overview and gives figures about how many police are in attendance and acts of violence perpetrated, if any. It turns a positive into a negative. In my opinion, Black achievements are minimised or ignored, just as they are in the film *Hidden Figures*, which demonstrates the pivotal role played by three female African American mathematicians in the astronaut John Glenn's launch into orbit. These types of films about Black people are so rare that when the film came out we immediately purchased a copy and made sure all our children saw it. When your children are brought up on a diet of negativity about their race on a daily basis - at school, in society and the media – we, as parents, try very hard to imbue into them some positive images about themselves. Hence the BBC acronym for Black children growing up in the UK – Black, British and Confused.

CHAPTER 7
Building a life together

"Do not die in the history of your past hurts and past experiences but live in the now and future of your destiny."
Michelle Obama

Outwardly, my husband's family and mine are polar opposites, as I have previously mentioned. Even now, after forty years of marriage, we receive reactions of surprise that we are a couple and have been together for so long. On the surface we appear to have very different personalities, but our fundamental beliefs, morals and values are very similar and from day one we were in agreement about how we would raise our children and instil those values in them.

We started married life in Manchester and had our children pretty quickly thereafter, so in many ways the children grew up with us. We both agreed that it was important that our children should understand their Caribbean culture. I shopped at the West Indian grocers, *Cariba*, which is based on Ayres Road, in Greater Manchester, and from there I purchased the Jamaican ackee that my husband loves, along with all the other ingredients needed for Caribbean meals such as yams, pumpkin, sweet potatoes, cassava and callaloo, so our children were used to eating Caribbean food and meals. When we visited Grandma Strachan in Preston, she would also cook Caribbean meals and bake her delicious cakes, which she was famous for in the town. Our children were also taught to cook at an early age, as were we. When their school friends visited and stayed overnight, they were always surprised when either Rhia or Ricky would cook breakfast or a meal. My mother and my husband's grandmother prepared us for life, and one important life skill was being able to cook good, healthy, tasty food that would nourish your body.

Other culturally rich events were the various Caribbean Carnivals held around the country. We would take the children to the Preston Caribbean Carnival, which is the largest and longest running cultural celebration in Preston, outside of the Preston Guild, and attracts thousands of visitors every year. My parents started taking me there as a little girl, Errol and I took our children there when they were little, and as an adult I would still go most years. There are elaborate costumes, parades, music that is evocative of the Caribbean, and stalls selling West Indian food. It is a time when people who have left Preston come back to celebrate and see friends and family; I like to attend Carnival to catch up with old friends and enjoy my Caribbean heritage. There are also bigger versions in Manchester and Leeds which we would also attend but the largest Carnival that we have ever attended is of course the annual Notting Hill Carnival in London.

Both Errol and I were brought up to attend church so both our children attended church schools, we went to Mass on Sundays, and at one point I was involved in the Sunday School class. As our children grew into teenagers, we left the decision to them as to whether or not they wanted to attend church and visits to church gradually tailed off. However, they still have the firm foundations and understanding of the teachings of the Bible. Both children were christened in church and took their First Communion. As a young girl I had my First Communion in Blackburn, whilst my daughter Rhia had hers in Urmston, near to where we then lived. On the day of her First Communion, I was sitting in the Church looking at the priest officiating the ceremony and I felt a jolt of recognition. I leaned over and whispered into my husband's ear, "I am sure that priest is Father Charnock who was at my first Communion Mass." My husband looked at me and shook his head. "I doubt it", he said. When the ceremony was over, I approached the priest and asked if he had ever been at St. Alban's Catholic School in Blackburn and he said yes, he had, and so strangely enough both my daughter and I have our First Communion pictures with the same priest standing behind us. Father Charnock was also one of the priests at my daughter's wedding.

Over the years our friends have praised our children because they were polite and well behaved. Part of this is because of their upbringing. As children, both Errol and I had to complete household chores, it wasn't optional. We had to dust the furniture, then mop and clean as we grew older, and learn to cook. I must admit that as I child I rarely saw my mum sit down. She was always doing something and if she did sit down, she would be sewing, or shelling peas. Mum didn't believe in being idle and her children were not allowed to be idle either! Errol and I had very similar upbringings which we passed on to our children; they had chores to do and would cook and bake frequently.

We encouraged our children to have hobbies and outside interests. Our daughter Rhia learned to play the violin and I remember one summer's day sitting outside in the garden, listening to her practice - it was wonderful. Learning to play an instrument is known to stimulate the brain cells and improve functions like memory and abstract reasoning. History repeats itself and recently my daughter sent me a video of my granddaughter, Sophia, playing the piano to an audience at school. My son Ricky like his father enjoys sport and keeping fit. From a young age he went cross country running, played cricket, basketball and football. A lot of weekends were spent with father and son attending football matches. Ricky loves football, he played professional football at high school for Crewe Alexandra and then semi-professional for a number of teams including Trafford and Flixton. He still plays amateur football on Saturdays and throughout the week. His daughter, Zendaya, spends hours looking at his medals and is now playing football herself and has her first medal.

We also instilled a strong work ethic in our children. They had paper rounds and as they got older and started asking for designer clothes and trainers, we encouraged them to get jobs to fund their expensive habits themselves. The Trafford Centre shopping mall opened near to where we lived, when they were teenagers, and both children had Saturday and weekend jobs there. To further develop their work ethic, Errol and I would take the children to 'bring your children to work' initiatives and both children were involved in my business for many years, where they honed their business skills and used their own creativity to contribute to my business. Rhia joined the business and took care of all the HR issues for my company, Olive Strachan Resources, and Ricky took care of sales and marketing for the company. I was fortunate to have two such fabulous brains within my organisation. They have both gone on to achieve success in their respective fields. I am proud to say that Rhia is now Director of People and Organisational Development at The Shrewsbury and Telford Hospital NHS Trust, and is married to Anthony Boyode with whom she has a daughter, Sophia. Ricky is Head of Sales – UK & South Africa for an organisation called Infront, and has three daughters, Mya, Zendaya and Ezrah, and married his fiancée, Serayna Eldrige, in Portugal in 2023. We are very proud of our children and grandchildren.

Juggling many roles

As part of my research into the prime of life, an article from the online magazine *Prime Women* asks the question "What is Prime and Prime for what exactly?" They argue that a woman does not hit her stride until her fifties when the childbearing twenties, thirties, and forties are in the rear-view mirror. Like most working mothers in the 1980s most of the day-to-day childcare was on my shoulders. I have a wonderful husband, who had no problem changing nappies, wiping noses, bathing, and reading to the children, but generally sorting out the children fell to me, as their mother. During the period when I was a stay-at-home mum, when the children were very young, Errol would arrive home from work and because I had been at home all day I would immediately start talking to him. He would say "Just give me a few minutes to wind down," and would go and watch the news or read the newspaper. I am a very independent person but I need the company of others to stimulate me and I found it hard to depend on one adult for conversation. I loved my children and felt privileged to have brought two beautiful, healthy, and joyful children into this world, but spending every day with two small children and no adults to talk to was hard, and I was keen to keep on working. Like any young couple with two children and a rented house, two wages were better than one and getting a job would be good for me as well as our finances, so I decided to look for a job. It was soul destroying. I left school with six 'O' Levels and had a BTEC Diploma in business studies but now I also had two young children, so not the most attractive proposition to employers, especially in those days. I remember attending one interview where the manager asked me if I was capable of working through the whole day, after staying at home with two children. My mouth fell open in shock! Anyone who has children will know that having a toddler and a baby in nappies does not make you a lady of leisure. I faced many rejections until finally an old friend from my recruitment days contacted me about a part-time position and from there I found a full-time role.

The next hurdle was organising suitable childcare. I went through the proper channels and found a registered childminder who came highly recommended. I was lucky and over the years had two wonderful ladies who cared for my children and gave them lots of love. Every morning Errol would leave for work early, as he had to drive to Glossop. I would then get the children ready, put them into a double buggy and run to the childminder's house. I then ran to catch my bus, which normally delivered me to work with just minutes to spare. If the children were sick, I would get a phone call and have to leave work, pick them up from school and take them home. Most days, as soon as work finished, I would run to the bus stop, run to the childminders, get the children home and start cooking the evening meal, then make sure their clothes, etc. were ready for the following day. My routine varied very little. Weekends involved catching up with the housework and ironing on Sunday. It wasn't all tedious housework and no play, we would go out as a family for walks in the countryside, or to art galleries, and sometimes we took the children to plays at the theatre. We had a good family life and as the children grew, we enjoyed eating all our meals sitting at the table together, with the television off, discussing the events of the day. My life was typical of any working mother. This was in the 1980s but a report by the BBC, published 18 May 2021 entitled *The hidden load: How thinking of everything holds mums back*, discusses the hidden work that mothers take on. It goes on to describe three overlapping categories: the cognitive labour – thinking about all the practical elements of household responsibilities, e.g., organising playdates, shopping, and planning activities; the emotional labour - maintaining the family's emotion, calming things down, worrying about how the children are managing at school, etc; and finally the mental load - the intersection of the two: preparing, organising and anticipating both emotional and practical issues that need to get done to make life flow. This really resonates with me; the role of a mother does not seem to have changed or advanced in any way over the years.

I had no regrets about returning to full time employment. I love the world of work, making new friends and waking up in the morning with a purpose, and eventually, with both of us working, we were able to save and apply for a mortgage. We purchased a house in Flixton, in the Borough of Trafford, Greater

PRIME

Manchester. I loved our beautiful home. Being married to an engineer meant that he practically rebuilt the house, putting in the central heating himself, bathroom fittings, etc., and completely decorating throughout. When the house was completed, Errol turned his hand to the garden. Our garden was so lovely that we received many comments and compliments from the neighbours. We lived in Flixton for twenty-eight years, our children grew up and went to school there. Eventually I learnt to drive and passed my driving test and then purchased my first car - the feeling of freedom it gave me was incredible.

I am married to an extremely ambitious and focused man. Early on in our marriage, when Rhia was two years old and our son Ricky just nine months, Errol went to Newcastle to study for a qualification which would help him in his future career. I did feel resentful at first. He was away during the week having some freedom, whereas I was left in Manchester with two small children until he came home at weekends. At the time I was not happy about him being away but in the long term the family benefited because as he became more qualified in his field, his salary grew commensurate with his knowledge and expertise. He went on to study for two master's degrees, one in building services engineering and one in electrical engineering. This meant that during the summer holidays, when we would normally have summer holidays away, Errol was constantly studying. You can imagine my reaction to this. It was a bone of contention between us for quite a while. From my perspective his ambition meant he did not have time for me and the children. But from his point of view, he knew that when he had achieved his goal, the whole family would benefit in the long run.

Eventually Errol's qualifications led him to the job of his dreams as a global executive for Reuters, but this meant him moving to London to live during the week. I remember helping my husband to move to his new London apartment, which he was sharing with a very attractive younger woman.

Understandably, I was concerned. However, moving to London was not right for the family. The children were settled, I was running my business, it wasn't practical to disrupt the whole family for his new job. There is a saying by German philosopher Friedrich Nietzsche "What doesn't kill you, makes you stronger"! At the beginning of this new living arrangement I was very lonely and I remember thinking, what is the point of being married if your husband is never with you? The children were considerably older by then, and although I wasn't happy about seeing my husband only at weekends, I grew accustomed to our way of life.

CHAPTER 8
A resilient marriage

On 19 June 2022, Errol and I celebrated 40 years of marriage. One of the questions that I am constantly asked is, "How have you managed it?" Looking at the statistics from the Marriage Foundation, in an article by Harry Benson, dated 15 December 2019, he states that "Half of marriages will end within 40 years, the majority through divorce rather than death." I feel lucky to have sustained my marriage for this long. When anyone enquires about the secret of a good marriage, I would say it is about tolerance, patience, compromise and allowing your partner to fulfil their dreams. Every marriage is different. When Errol started working away, a good friend of mine was horrified and stated "I wouldn't let my husband do that!" But then there were aspects of her marriage that I would not be happy with. There is no blueprint for any relationship, you work around it to fit yourselves.

From 2001 to 2018 Errol worked abroad. It started with Reuters and later he worked in Qatar, Shanghai, Saudi Arabi, and finally in Ireland. After working for Reuters, where he specialised in Data Centre Design, my husband made a reputation for himself in this field and was sought after. He was a consultant and worked for various organisations on long term contracts. His good friend Tosh Asueni was with him in Qatar and when he went to work in Saudi Arabi his friend Laurie Brown was also there. All three of them had studied engineering together and had remained friends.

Errol worked for Reuters for six years and although he was based in London, his job encompassed visiting their sites in over sixty countries. It was a demanding role, but he relished it. After the first year or so of complaining to everyone who would listen about how unhappy I was with this arrangement, I gave myself a good talking to and decided to find a solution to the problem. How could I make this work? Essentially I was lonely and I felt quite abandoned, as by then my children were doing their own thing and had their own lives. Fortunately, I am extremely resilient and adaptable and over time I became stronger and less dependent on my husband.

Nor did we allow ourselves to drift apart. Most days we spoke to each other via Skype, and at weekends Errol would sit with a cup of coffee wherever he was in the world, and I would sit with a coffee in the UK, and we would switch the camera on and just talk, sometimes for hours. In this way we kept abreast of each other's lives, the ups and downs, highs and lows. There was also some allowance for Errol to return home every few months or so. I would use my holidays from work to spend time with him, so that between us we were able to keep our relationship on track, and I visited Errol in Qatar and Shanghai.

I am blessed with some amazing girlfriends who really rallied around me during this time. I sent out messages to my women friends telling them I was available for days out, walks in the park, weekends away, meals out, etc., and the invitations came in. I was invited to a *Take That* concert by my friend at the last minute, when one of her group couldn't make it. The concert was at the Etihad Stadium in 2017, part of the band's Wonderland Tour, and we had a fabulous night. Many of my friends are single, divorced, or widowed, and I was never short of company. I visited China, Russia, and New Zealand with one of my friends, Jan Lewin. My sister in-law, Patricia (Pat) Strachan and I became very close and spent a great deal of time together, going to Leeds Carnival every year. My social calendar was full, with walks in the Lake District, lunches out with my girlfriends, trips to the theatre, spa weekends etc., and although I missed my husband, I had created a happy and fulfilling life for myself. That is why I have called this section of my book "a resilient marriage", because having been with Errol since I was nineteen years old, I had grown to depend on him quite heavily. He is my friend and life partner and knows all my faults and still loves me. When he went away it left a huge void in my life. In earlier years, most evenings after the children had gone to bed, we would sit and chat for hours about our life, our goals and aspirations. We would play gin rummy, backgammon or Scrabble until late into the evening, sharing a glass of wine or Errol's favourite, Tia Maria, and my favourite, a glass of Bailey's Irish Cream. It was a difficult transition for me but like every challenge I face in life, I always create a plan of action, decide what I want, and put steps in place to achieve my goal. That is why I grew stronger and more self-reliant during this period of my marriage.

CHAPTER 9
Prime for business

For people in business, our prime comes later. The way I see it, in your 20's you don't know anything. In your 30's you're ramping up, preparing. By your 40's and early 50's, usually, you're in your prime of working life. That's when you make the greatest impact.
Article by Plain English, 22 August 2019

My first job as a wife and mother was working in the recruitment industry. My daughter Rhia was six months old and I was looking for work. I made an appointment to see a recruitment agency called Brook Street in Manchester, hoping they could assist in my hunt for suitable employment. I walked into the agency with Rhia in my arms and was greeted by Jenny Hilditch, the branch manager at the time. She was warm and welcoming and immediately asked if she could hold my daughter for me whilst I completed the necessary documentation. Rhia was happy to go to her, and as I sat down to complete the paperwork, I could see other members of staff cooing over Rhia. She was laughing as members of the small team of staff held out their hands to give my daughter a cuddle. For me, being a stay-at-home mum at the time, it was just great to be out of the house and having a conversation with women of my own age group. I was there for hours as I made a connection with the team working there. I had all the necessary nappies and bottles for my daughter and she soon fell asleep in her pram whilst I chatted with the staff over coffee and biscuits. I really felt at home and was sorry when I had to leave.

At that time we didn't have a telephone at home, but I had given them my neighbour's number so the agency could contact me regarding job vacancies. The following day, my neighbour ran across to my house, brimming with excitement on my behalf. The agency was on the phone and wanted to speak to me about a job! I ran to her house, answering the phone breathlessly. Jenny Hilditch wanted me to come in for an interview to work as part of her team in the recruitment agency. I couldn't believe it! After so many "no's" I had felt that at twenty-one years old I was unemployable, and my confidence had hit rock bottom. Now, after so many rejections - rejected because I was the wrong colour, rejected because I didn't have the right qualifications, rejected because I had a young baby – someone was willing to give me a chance.

My interview was successful and I began my career in the recruitment industry which would span eleven years. My role was to interview and test job seekers in order to create a pool of people ready to fill vacancies. I had to match candidates to suitable jobs, screen and shortlist candidates before employers interviewed them, and meet company targets for the number of vacancies taken or people placed in jobs. This role required a high level of skill, as we were dealing with some of the largest organisations in Manchester. Our clients were either managers, directors, or HR managers. To prepare me for my new job I was sent away to a hotel for a week's training, where every day we had a full day's workshop, with some revision work in the evening, and an exam at the end of the course.

I absolutely loved every minute! Rhia was being taken care of by her doting daddy, who she adored, so I was free to absorb the learning. When I returned to the branch in Manchester, I immediately demonstrated an aptitude for extracting the salient details from the organisation with the vacancy, finding the right candidate to match their requirements, and putting the two together successfully. I was paid a basic salary but for every person I placed in a job role and who remained there for twelve weeks minimum, I received commission. Soon I was earning good money and Jenny was so pleased she'd recruited me.

I remained at Brook Street until I had my son Ricky in 1984. When Ricky was six months old, Errol was temporarily out of work and he looked after the children when I got a job at Sight and Sound Secretarial College on Princess Street. It was mainly an administrative role, which I didn't really enjoy. Fortunately, my good friend Rita Logan was based at Reed Employment on King Street and I went back into the recruitment industry with relief, soon to become a valuable part of the team. Over the next nine years or so, I worked for a variety of agencies. I helped to open the first branch of ADECCO on Deansgate and my final role in recruitment was working for Blue Arrow, where I managed a team, and was also a regional coach for other branches, helping new managers achieve success.

During my years in recruitment, I had many conversations with HR managers, understanding the issues they faced and trying to find the right staff for their organisations. I also had regular meetings with directors, managers, and business owners. Before I could source the right staff for them, I had to understand their business, how it worked and issues they were facing. This gave me insight into a range of industries, building relationships with key influential leaders in Manchester.

OLIVE STRACHAN MBE

The IRA bomb

I love the City of Manchester and lived there from the age of twenty until I was fifty-nine years old. Most of the important and memorable moments in my life took place there. The people of Manchester, "Mancunians", have their own brand of warmth and I would walk around the City Centre on my own, feeling quite safe. Often complete strangers smiled and acknowledged my presence with a nod of the head, a wave, or just a friendly grin. One of my favourite squares to sit in and contemplate life is St Anne's Square, at the heart of Manchester's shopping district, not only home to exclusive shops but also to the Royal Exchange Theatre, bars, and restaurants. Frequently, when I sit there just enjoying the ambiance, someone will engage me in conversation, a complete stranger just passing the time of day.

Manchester has been good to me and my family. It is where I established and grew my business, and where my two children grew up to be strong, confident adults, and where three of my granddaughters were born. It is where my husband launched his career as a life scientist engineer, and it is a fabulous city for work, rest and play. Reading travel information about why Manchester is a great city to visit, the University of Manchester's website article, *Multicultural Manchester*, describes it as "One of the most multicultural cities in the UK, with nearly 200 languages spoken there". Over the years the city has grown and evolved, offering entertainment, theatre, restaurants, great shopping and excellent food and drink. Living in this vibrant city means that there is always something amazing to do and if I was ever bored at the weekend I would just search online for "things to do in Manchester at the weekend", and a whole smorgasbord of suggestions would arrive at my fingertips. When I had the grandchildren staying with me for the weekend we would pore over the list together, selecting our adventure for the day.

There was a time when the beautiful city of Manchester was ravaged by an IRA bomb. In the 1980s I worked on King Street, now one of the premium shopping destinations in Manchester, with over forty big-name brands, diverse bars and restaurants but in the 1980s it consisted of retail shops, bakeries, jewellers, etc. Over the years Manchester has been the target of many bomb scares. I remember on one occasion I was working in an upstairs office on King Street, for an agency called Premier Employment, when suddenly there was a noise from the street below. A policeman was speaking though a loudspeaker, announcing that there was a bomb scare and they would be evacuating us from our buildings. We all had to wait inside until we were given permission to leave. I remember we all huddled together in the office, absolutely terrified. Finally, we were allowed to leave and we all piled into Collette Gordon's car, as she'd parked closest to the office, and we shook like leaves until we had left the environs of the city centre. This happened more than once, so Mancunians became used to bomb scares being announced to the point that we became a little blasé about it. "Oh, not another one!", we would say.

PRIME

But on 15 June 1996 something terrible happened that I will never forget. This is a report of the devastating event by Jennifer Williams, 15 June 2016, for The Manchester Evening News:

"It was a day Manchester will never forget.
On June 15, 1996, the IRA singled out our city to be victim of the biggest bomb it had ever exploded on the British mainland.
It would injure hundreds and leave no building within half a mile unscathed.
This was a blast that tore through the heart of Manchester and which, within seconds, would have an impact that would last for two decades.
The day started in blazing midsummer sunshine.
Two hundred miles south in London, anti-terror police were on high alert amid fears the IRA could target the Queen's Trooping the Colour parade.
In Manchester things were more relaxed. But police were nonetheless prepared for trouble – as thousands of football fans prepared to pour into town ahead of that afternoon's Euro 96 match between England and Scotland.
TV crews from across Europe were in town to cover the next day's Russia v Germany game at Old Trafford. Thousands of shoppers were preparing to hit the streets too, many of them on the look-out for Father's Day gifts.
Unknown and unnoticed a white van was already on its devastating journey.
Just before 9.20am, the streets had already begun filling up with crowds when two men in hooded anoraks and sunglasses left a heavily loaded Ford Cargo van outside Marks and Spencer on the corner of Cannon Street and Corporation Street. It was parked on double yellow lines with its hazard lights flashing.
It contained 3,300lbs of homemade explosive, three times the size of the Canary Wharf bomb.
They walked away, ringing an IRA chief in Ireland to let them know the job was done. The pair escaped in a burgundy Ford Granada, later abandoned in Preston.
Three minutes after the van was abandoned, a traffic warden slapped a ticket on it.
Some time after 9.38am a man with an Irish accent called Granada TV, Sky News, Salford University, North Manchester General Hospital and the Garda police in Dublin to warn a bomb would go off in one hour. He gave the location and used a code word known to Special Branch.
On their CCTV camera in Bootle Street station, officers watched in horror as footage was relayed showing people pushing up against and sliding along the side of the van, awkwardly parked on one of the city's busiest shopping streets.
Officers then began one of the most extraordinary policing operations the country has ever seen: the evacuation of 80,000 people.
At first, they were not keen to go. Mancunians had become used to bomb scares and they had things to be getting on with.

OLIVE STRACHAN MBE

One hairdresser refused to let his clients leave because they still had chemicals in their hair, arguing it would be 'too dangerous'. A group of workmen wanted to stay put because they were on weekend rates.

It was a Herculean task, aided by the luck of having extra police on duty for the match. Gradually, grudgingly, people began to move, turning into a flood as word spread that the scare was real. The police cordon extended out and out to a quarter of a mile, until there were no more officers to take it any further.

By 11.10am, the heart of Manchester city centre was deserted. Only one or two people were still within the exclusion zone, having somehow escaped knowledge of the evacuation.

When the bomb exploded, the blast could be heard from 15 miles away. It issued a force so powerful it travelled around 90-degree corners, knocking people to the ground and blowing out virtually every window within half a mile, leaving a 15m crater around it.

Glass rained from the sky: a fine dust followed by shards and eventually a torrent of rubble and debris. From his vantage point on Cross Street, Chief Inspector Ian Seabridge later recalled that there was then a 'sudden air of stillness'."

We were fortunate, because as a family we had planned to go into Manchester city centre do so some shopping but at the last minute our son Ricky mentioned that he was playing the drums in a concert at his school, St. Antony's Roman Catholic School in Urmston. We heard the explosion from Urmston which is approximately ten miles from the city centre. Later, when we watched the local evening news, we realised just how lucky we were not to go shopping that day. There were over 200 people injured, although luckily no fatalities. The reported traumas came from the shattering of thousands of windows and other damage to buildings, which had a long-term impact. An article in *The Manc*, a publication which claims to be the people's voice of Greater Manchester, published on 15 June 2023, marked twenty-seven years since the explosion, and said that "It is estimated that the bomb caused an estimated £700 million worth of damage to Manchester's infrastructure and economy". It was a challenging time for individuals and businesses but there was also a feeling of togetherness, looking out for each other, and working together to rebuild.

More recently our family once again had a lucky escape from another Manchester bombing. Our eldest granddaughter, Mya, was supposed to attend the Ariana Grande concert with her friends, on 22 May 2017, but she couldn't. She was so disappointed not to be able to go, however, just moments after Ariana Grande finished the final song, a suicide bomber detonated an explosion at the Manchester Arena, killing twenty-two concertgoers and injuring 116 more. The Islamic state, ISIS, claimed responsibility for what was the deadliest act of terrorism in Britain since the 2005 London Metro bombings. When you see the terror and carnage caused by the bombing on TV, and the reconstruction of what happened, I just have to thank God that Mya wasn't there, whilst my heart goes out to all the families who suffered as a consequence.

Manchester was in mourning once again. A report in the *Manchester Evening News* dated 26 May 2017, by Katie Butler and Joe Thomas, titled *The astonishing sea of flowers in St Ann's Square is still growing*, said that more than 4,000 touching tributes had been laid at the Manchester attack memorial in the city. Mourners stood at the edge of the floral display, which also included balloons and teddy bears alongside photographs of the twenty-two people killed. Errol and I visited St Ann's Square to pay our respects. This moving tribute of a sea of flowers, like a carpet covering the square, was as beautiful as it was poignant. There was not a dry eye to be seen.

1996 was not only a year for personal and professional upheaval in my life, with the long-term impact of the bombing in Manchester but I was also ready for the next phase of my working life. I felt I had gone as far as I was going to go in recruitment. I wanted to advance to the top of the industry, but I was informed that without a degree I could go no further than being a manager. I had a long working life ahead of me and decided that I needed to make sure that I was attractive to future employers. I made some enquires and concluded that it would make sense to build on my career. Rather than start again, I felt that my knowledge of the recruitment industry would stand me in good stead for a career in Human Resources, so I enrolled to study at Salford University for a Post Graduate Diploma in Human Resource Management. This was a seminal moment in my life. University opened a world of learning that I had not tapped into before, it boosted my confidence and gave me credibility. It opened doors for me and changed my thinking, whilst creating opportunities that I had never dreamed of.

I established relationships and made new friends with whom I am still in contact more than twenty-five years later. I became an Associate Member of my local branch of the Chartered Institute of Personnel and Development (CIPD) which introduced me to other professionals, and attending their events helped to develop my skills. Being amongst HR and Learning & Development professionals meant that I had mentors and coaches who could assist in my growth and development. Eventually I was appointed the first Black female Chair of the Manchester branch of the CIPD.

Whilst I was studying part-time and working full-time, Video Arts, an award-winning e-learning provider, famous for delivering corporate training in an entertaining and memorable way, placed a vacancy for a manager to open and establish their new local office in Salford. I put myself forward and had to attend an interview in London with a presentation to the board of directors. It was nerve-wracking, but I was successful! It was as though the stars had aligned! I was studying HR, which included learning and development, and I was now working in an organisation famous for corporate training. I had pivoted into an industry which ultimately would help me achieve my goal in working to develop the skills and capabilities of organisations and individuals.

After working in the recruitment industry, which at the time was female dominated, working for Video Arts posed many challenges. I was now working in a mainly male dominated environment. Recruitment at the time consisted of completing most documents by hand, whereas Video Arts was moving towards digital and e-learning. I had to learn new skills and working methodology. A big part of my role was making presentations to clients and attending trade shows. It was a very visible role. I also grew my contact base; many of Video Arts' clients were large organisations like Shell UK, GlaxoSmithKline and Cussons International, who had large training budgets to spend. My job was to provide guidance on the most beneficial way of spending their training budget. This meant that I had to keep abreast of the training market so that my clients could look on me as someone who was knowledgeable and able to give good advice. Often a client would give us their training needs analysis, a process that identifies the training and development needs of individuals and the organization, together with the company's competency framework, which defines the knowledge, skills and attributes that employees need to have if they are to perform successfully, and together with my team of staff we would prepare a spreadsheet recommending resources to meet their specific needs.

The social life at Video Arts was second to none because their videos starred actors such as John Cleese, Dawn French and Hugh Laurie, to name a few, and when they had staff conventions or parties the stars would be in attendance. At one of these events I had the pleasure of meeting John Cleese, Dawn French, and Lennie Henry, who was attending with his wife at the time. I loved my job but like all good things it came to an end when they decided to centralise the functions in London and close the regional offices.

In 1998 two momentous things happened. Firstly, I passed my Post Graduate Diploma in Human Resource Management! It was an amazing feeling, dressed in cap and gown with my friends who had supported me and been my study buddies for three years, throwing our caps in the air in celebration! Secondly, after I was made redundant by Video Arts, I applied for several jobs and was told that at thirty-seven I was too old, so I decided that I would fulfil my ambition and work for myself. I had my husband's blessing and support, and Errol suggested that because I had worked in recruitment for many years and subsequently for Video Arts, my name was well known in the business community and I should call my company *Olive Strachan Resources*. The business was in two parts: a resource centre with viewing facilities offering videos, CD's, books, games, and simulations for training (we were agents for Video Arts, the BBC, The Industrial Society, etc.), and delivery of training, coaching and mentoring services, event and conference speaking. We offered design and delivery of training or clients could rent or buy training resources from our centre.

PRIME

I am often asked the question as to how I managed to sustain a business, my marriage, and bring up two children. During the first three years of my business being established, Errol was still working in the UK and he was my first accountant until he pursued his international career. By this time my daughter, nineteen years old and my son, seventeen, were starting to find their own way in life, but I was always there when needed.

Fundamentally, when I locked the door at night, most evenings it would be just me, climbing the stairs to bed alone. It wasn't what I signed up for when I married. Yes, I could have rented our home and gone to join Errol abroad. I had been to visit him in Qatar, where his home was extremely glamorous and lovely, no expense spared for his comfort. We went to parties and I met the wives and girlfriends of other expats living there. Their husbands were out all day working, earning good salaries, so they could afford to have help in the home, which meant housework was not part of their remit anymore. However, most of them seemed bored, with life consisting of an endless round of parties and cocktails which really didn't appeal to me. I had a career of my own and an exciting growing business which I was not willing to give up.

Errol and I agreed that the best solution was for me to remain in the UK and fulfil my dreams, whilst he worked internationally and fulfilled his. During this period I faced many challenges. The office I was renting on Deansgate, Manchester, was broken into by someone under the influence of drugs, according to the police. I recruited an employee and when I later had to terminate her employment, she was very unhappy about it. I often worked very late, sometimes leaving my office at midnight which with hindsight wasn't the wisest thing to do. As I approached my car one evening, I could see it didn't look right, and as I got closer I saw that my tyres were flat, glass from a window was on the floor, and someone had made deep scratches into the paintwork. I had often given this employee a ride home, or taken her with me to client meetings, so she knew where I parked my car - and she had told me about the unsavoury characters in her family and boasted about the types of criminality they were involved in. Thankfully, I have never seen or heard from this person since.

The biggest crisis was when I returned from a meeting one day to find the bailiffs about to close the offices I was renting. Although I had paid my rent on time, as had every other company in the serviced offices, our landlord had not paid his rent. I had to find and move into new offices over a weekend, a very stressful time.

With all this happening and more, I had full, exciting, and busy life. The business evolved, I recruited staff, won an international contract, and travelled to places that I never in my wildest dreams thought I would see: Yemen, Uzbekistan, Serbia, Bangkok, to name a few. On the odd occasion I would be working in Qatar whilst Errol was based there. Errol had made friends out there, so we had some lovely evenings at the Souk and drives out into the desert - we were both being paid to travel the world!

From the age of thirty-seven onwards I started to feel a sense of vigour, and that I was making an impact. Up until this time I was not clear on what I wanted to achieve in my life but opening my own business gave me a laser sharp focus. I had to make this work.

Especially now, when I am moving toward the phase I call "living my prime", I reflect on the glorious journey that I have taken through working for myself. When I speak at seminars or coach entrepreneurs one of the main questions I'm asked is "How?" How did I achieve my goals and fulfil my professional dreams?

CHAPTER 10
Nurturing aspirations and fulfilling professional dreams

During the twenty-five years of running Olive Strachan Consultancy, I have worked with large organisations with 10,000 staff or more, medium sized organizations with up to 500 employees, to entrepreneurs who do not currently employ staff. I have worked in a variety of industries: football, with Everton Football Club; hospitality, with the TUI group; oil and gas with Tyco Wormald; pharmaceutical, with Astra Zeneca and GlaxoSmithKline, etc., but one of my largest clients, and one that I sustained a relationship with for twenty years, is the British Council, an organisation specialising in international cultural and educational opportunities.

My work has involved working with CEO's and directors, departments and teams, supervisors and individuals, delivering training, presenting, opening conferences, as well as coaching and mentoring.

To answer the question, how did I achieve my goals and what advice I would give to others, I have an acronym that I use when coaching entrepreneurs – KNOWLEDGE:

K – know your business, an idea is not enough. Often when I work with entrepreneurs who have a great idea, when I ask some key questions, for instance "What exactly are you offering? Who are your target clients? What is your plan for attracting them? How many other people are doing this? What is the competition?" Many of them cannot answer these questions. Before opening my consultancy, I had some knowledge of the HR field, having worked with HR professionals for over eleven years, listening to the positives and negatives of this profession. I had also worked in the training field, helping large corporate clients with their training needs analyses. To be credible I had to have some qualifications and so, whilst still working full time, I returned to university on a part-time evening basis to study for a Post Graduate Diploma in Human Resource Management. I built a name for myself for in the business community. I was also aware that most of the consultants that I'd met were white males aged fifty plus; there was a niche market for a late thirties Black woman! I exploited my difference to my advantage; it wasn't plain sailing because I was not quite what was expected as a consultant, however, I persevered and now there are many Black female consultants. I like to think that I was a forerunner of things to come.

N – Network, it is never too soon to get out there! Amy Danise editor of Forbes says, "I believe your network is your net worth"! The beauty of social media and the aftermath of Covid means that we know we can network sitting at our desk at home. My particular favourite is LinkedIn. If I review my last five contracts, they all came from being contacted via LinkedIn. You can network by joining a group that is pertinent to your industry, for example, I am part of an HR Community and an entrepreneur community on LinkedIn. Or just reach out to someone you would like to connect with, write a lovely note outlining why you would like to connect with them. This can be very effective.

When I first opened my consultancy, I knew that if I didn't get myself known as a consultant in the business community I was doomed to failure. I became a member of the CIPD which was so beneficial. I attended meetings and was able to meet seasoned consultants who had years of experience. I could listen to presentations regarding new developments in HR and I could hone my skills. Most importantly, I made new contacts. It just so happened that whilst attending one of these meetings I was offered a piece of work which lasted for six months. I also joined the Institute of Directors (IoD) - if I was going to work with Directors, I needed to understand the issues they faced and build relationships with them. I networked with a purpose, aligning myself with larger organisations who could help me to hone my skills as well as aid my growth and development.

O – Be open to innovation, have a growth mindset! I began my business as a Resource Centre offering training services but as customer demand changed, and video streaming became the norm, we pivoted into delivering training and speaking at events, from which clients then requested coaching and mentoring services. During the Covid pandemic, face to face delivery was no longer possible and so I adapted to provide remote training and speaking engagements via Zoom and other platforms. As we know, the impact of Zoom is that it is now normal to attend events remotely, permanently changing the way we work. If we do not keep abreast of what is happening and do not change appropriately, our business will not grow and may even become defunct.

W – Work with your figures or if accounting is not your strength find someone who is good at finances. For the first couple of years my husband was my company accountant, which is his area of strength. As the business grew, I then employed an accountant. In the UK you can be called by the tax office for a VAT inspection at any time. This has happened to me twice and it can be quite daunting as they examine your figures closely, looking for any irregularities. Thankfully for me, on both occasions my figures were in order with only minor queries. When it comes to business, my advice is, do what you do best and outsource the rest. I have banked with NatWest bank since opening my business, at which time I was allocated a relationship manager. Over the years, the bank has been instrumental in helping me make the best financial decisions for my business to grow and be successful.

I - Invest time in relationships. When you are in the throes of growing your business, you can get so caught up in being a successful entrepreneur that you neglect the important relationships in your life, be it partner, husband or family. Make them a priority, because running a business can be a lonely occupation. You need the people who love and care for you to be there for you, but it must be a two-way street. Client relationships are also precious and must be maintained and nurtured. Remembering important dates, calling them, not just about business but just to see how they are. Taking them out for lunch or a coffee. Spotting an interesting article or item of business that could be of interest to them and sending it to them. Showing that you care is important for all relationships.

E – Emotional Intelligence. Prior to starting my career in the HR/learning and development field, I had always believed that being super intelligent with a high IQ were the seeds to success in life. However, research by Daniel Goleman, the author of the best-selling book *Emotional Intelligence*, has shown that being able to understand and control your emotions, having some insight into the emotions of others and how your behaviour impacts on them is an important part of business, but it is also a life skill. While IQ (intelligence Quotient) is a measure of your ability to solve problems and think logically, EQ (Emotional Quotient) measures your ability to understand and manage emotions. Your EQ can have a greater influence on your success in life than your IQ.

D – Decide to be credible and inspire trust. When you are credible you are considered to be an expert in your field by exhibiting confidence and a high level of expertise. This is key in building a brand that has longevity. Research who the experts are in your field, find out what they are offering and how it compares to what you are offering. In my case, I realised that I had to gain the right qualifications in HR, hence completing my Post Graduate Diploma and then my masters in HR. Then I had to hone my skills by taking on challenging assignments, successfully working with large blue-chip organisations as well as smaller organisations to build my reputation. I had to overcome challenges and prove that I had a strategic goal and the drive to achieve it.

G - Generate growth through sales from answering the phone, communication by email, or attending an event. You are selling your brand. Keeping your current client base happy and attracting new ones is your *raison d'etre* when it comes to business. One of your main avenues for sales should be through recommendations, i.e., happy clients telling others how fabulous you are. Maintaining a sales pipeline is essential and you should have some idea where your next contract is coming from.

Keep up to date client information and keep in contact, keep networking, and follow up on any leads. Ideally you should have a salesperson doing this for you, but as most entrepreneurs are starting off small, you may have to do this yourself. Always Be Closing (ABC) – is a sales strategy where a person should constantly be looking to close a sale.

E - Ensure you remain visible; this is a lesson I had to learn the hard way. I have a strong social media presence on LinkedIn, Instagram, Facebook, and Twitter. At one point, I grew weary of constantly posting on social media and wondered what the point of it was? Someone actually thought that I was ill and commented "I've not seen you posting anything for a while, are you ok?" Also I saw a correlation between my lack of posting to the enquiries I was receiving regarding work contracts. Since then, I post regularly and make sure that I attend networking events on a regular basis. An entrepreneur who does not ensure that their product or service is celebrated is not likely to gain a share of the market or expand their business.

CHAPTER 11
Say no to the "pause"

It would be impossible to write a book about being in one's prime and not discuss a big transition in a woman's life called the menopause. At the time of writing this book, there is a big furore about a comment made by Don Lemon, Journalist and CNN host. He said, "A woman is considered to be in their prime in their 20's and 30's and maybe 40's"! His comments were met with immediate pushback from his female co-hosts and resounding scorn from critics. When challenged, Don Lemon blamed Google, he kept saying, "Just Google it!" As part of my research, I thought it would be good to see what our Artificial Intelligence natural language processing tool, ChatGPT, says about the menopause. I would say it is a very comprehensive overview, as follows.

ChatGPT - what is the menopause?
"Menopause is a natural biological process that marks the end of a woman's reproductive years. It is defined as the permanent cessation of menstruation, indicating the end of the menstrual cycle and fertility. Menopause occurs due to a gradual decline in the production of reproductive hormones, specifically estrogen and progesterone, by the ovaries.

The average age of menopause is around 51, but it can vary widely among women. Menopause is typically confirmed after 12 consecutive months without a menstrual period. However, leading up to menopause, women often experience a transitional phase called perimenopause, which can last several years.

During perimenopause and menopause, women may experience various physical and emotional symptoms due to hormonal fluctuations. Some common symptoms include hot flashes, night sweats, irregular periods, vaginal dryness, sleep disturbances, mood changes, decreased libido, and changes in urinary function. These symptoms can range from mild to severe, and their duration varies from woman to woman.

While menopause is a natural part of aging, it can have a significant impact on a woman's quality of life. Therefore, many women seek medical interventions to manage their symptoms. Hormone replacement therapy (HRT) is one such option, which involves taking medications containing hormones to replace those that the body no longer produces. Other treatments, such as lifestyle changes, alternative therapies, and medications targeted at specific symptoms, may also be recommended.

It's important to note that menopause does not signify the end of a woman's overall health or well-being. With proper medical care and self-care practices, women can lead healthy and fulfilling lives after menopause. Regular check-ups with healthcare professionals, a balanced diet, regular exercise, and emotional support can all contribute to maintaining overall health during and after menopause."

Is it hot in here or is it me?

This was my constant refrain when I became impacted by the menopause during my late forties. I was fortunate not to have all the symptoms listed in the ChatGPT article, however, I did experience some. The worst and most embarrassing one to me was the change in my body temperature. I would be sitting in a meeting with a client and suddenly beads of sweat would form on my forehead and trickle down my face. I had no control over this, my method of dealing with it was to pretend that nothing was happening. I did receive some odd looks on occasion. I remember a young man pointing out to me that I was perspiring, and I replied "Yes, I know, because it is happening to me!"

Another symptom were the hot sweats at night. Sleep was impossible as I tossed and turned, trying to find a cool spot in the bed. My husband was working away at the time so I suffered alone, but when he did come home for a visit he was affected by my restlessness and inability to sleep. I think on those occasions he felt like he was experiencing the menopause with me.

One of the worst symptoms was forgetfulness, which led me to panic one day when I was walking around Flixton, not far from my home. For a moment I didn't know where I was. I was completely disorientated and wasn't sure I would be able to find my way home. I stood still, closed my eyes and concentrated, and gradually everything came into focus. Unwittingly I dropped my brand-new iPhone during the moment of panic, which didn't become apparent until I got home and tried to call my children. I searched everywhere and then realised that I must have dropped it whilst walking. Just as I was wondering what I could do, my son rang me on the landline and explained that he had called me on my mobile and a strange woman had answered. She explained that she had found my phone and gave him her phone number and address so I could collect it from her that same evening. When things like this happen, it restores your faith in human nature. I drove to her house that evening, taking wine and chocolates as a thank you.

The menopause did impact on my work. Once, whilst making a speech, I completely lost my train of thought so I asked the audience "Now where was I?"

and they reminded me! People can be very forgiving because we are all human after all. Another instance was when I was booked to deliver a training session and arrived the day before to prepare. I remember getting out of bed, my training plan and exercises on the table in front of me. I looked at the clock and it said 9am. I sat there ruminating and before I knew it, the time was 11am. I had lost two hours, lost in thought. This was a strange phenomenon for me.

I spoke about my experiences with my girlfriends, and received some good advice about wearing light clothes, taking supplements such as Black Cohosh, and avoiding alcohol and coffee which seemed to exacerbate the problem. It wasn't unusual for me to get only two or three hours' sleep at night, which certainly had an impact on my brain function. I had arranged to meet a client at the Midland Hotel in Manchester, one of my favourite venues. I woke up feeling slightly dizzy but after breakfast was feeling much better. As I sat waiting for my client in the foyer, suddenly I saw flickering lights coming from my peripheral vision. The lights formed into little triangles joined together and started to shimmer. Once again, I felt dizzy. I looked up, trying to ease the intensity of this experience, but it became worse as the lights from the edge of my vison merged with the lights from the chandeliers of the foyer, so that everything around me seemed to shimmer and merge. I sat still as my heart rate accelerated in fear. I closed my eyes again and concentrated on remaining calm, not sure what to do. I wanted to go to the ladies' bathroom and splash cold water on my face but was frightened that if I stood up the dizziness might cause me to fall over, which was just too humiliating to contemplate. Gradually, the lights faded and my vision returned to normal, and I was able to conclude my meeting with no further mishap. These ocular migraines happened to me on a few occasions when I had prolonged periods without sleep.

Another time, I had to deliver a presentation at a Road Show for Astra Zeneca in Macclesfield, Cheshire. I took great pride in providing my clients with an excellent service and waking up that morning after only three hours of sleep, I had the familiar dizzy feeling and the lights flashing around my peripheral vision. I did feel a sense of panic, because in two hours I was supposed to be delivering a session on motivation to an audience of 100 people and what's more, I had to deliver the same session four times that day. Calling and cancelling was out of the question. To give me time to rest my eyes and prepare, I ordered a taxi instead of driving myself and lay my head back against the seat, breathing deeply and thinking calm thoughts. The dancing lights in my vision continued for the 45-minute journey. However, as I walked into the room allocated to me for the event the lights stopped flashing and my vision returned to normal. I was so relieved that I was able to perform well and not let my client down, and I received great feedback. I know there are many women who have had to work through days when they just wanted to stay in bed but when you work for yourself and have a reputation to maintain, there is often no choice.

The menopause is not a disease; it is a rite of passage. Throughout the time of my experience, it was not talked about openly in the workplace. Thankfully, times have changed and now we have podcasts from people like Oprah Winfrey about how you can deal with the symptoms etc. HR departments are writing policies to encompass the menopause. There are support groups on social media and diet gurus who concentrate on eating well whilst you go through this transition. The CIPD has created a guide called *The menopause at work: A guide for people professionals*. It encourages organisations to treat the menopause like any other health issue and break the stigma attached to it.

How I dealt with the menopause

When my symptoms first began I visited my doctor and had some tests. They revealed that I was experiencing the perimenopause, which I was told could last for a number of years. I didn't want to start on any medication that I would have to keep taking for a prolonged period of time so I decided to treat this as any other problem in my life. I researched the most informative books available at the time. I have always admired Dr. Miriam Stoppard and found her book *Menopause* really informative. In it she says "The menopause is an important crossroads in your life and if viewed positively, it can be a rewarding and revealing one." After reading this book I felt fully prepared for what was ahead of me, as all the information required is in this fabulous book.

Secondly, I wanted a book that would help me with the emotional aspect of the menopause and a friend recommended Sue Monk Kidd's *When the Heart Waits*, described as being an excellent source of text for those who are on a personal spiritual journey. Monk Kidd, encountering a mid-life crisis, writes about her transformation of spirit. Both books gave me what I needed and after reading them I felt able to take control of my journey through the menopause.

The whole experience lasted about five years. My husband said that I was short tempered and hard to live with some of the time, which I accept. When you are mentally and physically challenged and your body is behaving in a way that is totally foreign to you, every day seems like an effort to appear normal and keep going. I would describe it as being alone in a little boat on the ocean during a storm. The waves are huge, making the boat rock until it is nearly capsizing, and you are covered from head to toe in cold water. The sharks are circling ready to gobble you up at any moment and you haven't slept or eaten for days. You are just hanging on by your fingertips hoping the storm will pass and you will soon be on dry land. When you feel like this, there is not much left in you to give to anyone else, most days I was just trying to get through. Thankfully, I am on the other side of it now and feel much more in control of both my physical and mental state.

My advice would be that if you suspect that you are experiencing the menopause, see your doctor. Knowing is better than guessing. Ask about what they can recommend. Speak to friends and family, share the experience, everyone will have their own individual stories and suggestions. Complete your own research, there are so many podcasts, articles and books available now. When you have completed all your research, decide what is best for you.

CHAPTER 12
Life's rich tapestry

In 1990 we purchased what we thought would be our 'forever' home in Flixton, Manchester. It was the house of my dreams, on a long, tree-lined street, with a beautiful garden at the back. Errol was working for Trafford Borough Council at the time and had spotted the house on his travels. It was not too far from the motorway, near good schools and a park around the corner.

Our happiness was only dented by the legal costs associated with purchasing a house, and the cost of childcare. Our children were eight and six years old, both still at primary school. Within two years the interest rates rose to 15% and we were barely able to pay our mortgage. Our only other large outgoing was food. I searched for books with titles such as *Living Frugally* and *Recipes for Those Living on a Budget*. I bought mincemeat because it was cheaper and I could make five meals out of it: spaghetti Bolognaise, meatballs, lasagne, chilli, and meat pie. Understandably, the children would say "Not mince again!" I remember Ricky asking for jam on his toast, and I had to tell him that we didn't have any jam. It was a hard time for us. Errol had a Ford Escort which we couldn't afford to have fixed, and we lived on a hill so we had to push it to get it started. Errol would drive and the children and I would push and then jump in! The neighbours must have thought we were like the Clampetts from *The Beverly Hillbillies*! Although financially we were strapped for cash, we loved the area and our children soon made friends and were happy.

Errol is the most capable man that I know, he can turn his hand to anything. He fitted all our central heating and decorated the house more than once over the twenty-eight years we lived there. He fitted wooden flooring and did the tiling, and he decorated the outside of the house, including fixing roof tiles when needed. Errol is also a keen gardener and we always had beautiful lawns. At Christmas time we had a tree in the front garden which Errol would decorate with lights every year, as well as decorating the whole house with Christmas lights. We had lots of compliments from our neighbours regarding his artistic decorations. When Errol started to work abroad, I remember a little boy from across the road coming to ask me when he was returning as he missed the lights on the house and the tree in the garden. I was okay with decorating inside the house but living on my own when the children had left home, I didn't feel motivated to spend hours decorating the house for Christmas.

As the years passed the interest rate went down and life settled into a routine. The children grew up, finished school, and went to university. We had some lovely neighbours: Jean Fairclough, who kept an eye on the children for us if for any reason we were late back from work; Bridie and Jimmy, who were the first people to welcome us when we moved in; and Rachel and Gerald, our next-door neighbours, who were friendly and supportive. We kept on working hard and our fortunes changed for the better. Our life improved considerably when Errol became a Global Executive for Reuters. This was his dream job, travelling around the world as a consultant, using his knowledge as an engineer in an advisory capacity. At the same time my own business took off and we started to reap the rewards of our hard work. We had two holidays a year, one in Europe and then a holiday in the Caribbean during winter so that we could start the year in the sunshine.

We were able to invest in top of the range cars, Errol with a BMW, and me with a Mercedes. I must admit I loved my car. It was dark blue with a white leather interior, and complete strangers often commented on what a beautiful car it was. On long drives the car would just glide down the motorway. I named it Maximillian, a name fitting for such magnificence, and we had many conversations during my trips to London. I was so attached to the car that I kept it for fourteen years and only changed it when the garage said that it would cost more to fix it than the car was worth.

Eventually, our mortgage was paid off and we were enjoying life. Manchester is a beautiful city and we made the most of it. I visited the theatre with Errol but mostly with my girlfriends, going to concerts where we saw Luther Vandross, Tina Turner, Lionel Ritchie, Alexander O' Neal, to name a few. We saw musicals such as Miss Saigon, South Pacific, The Lion King, Mama Mia, 9-5, etc. And we enjoyed meals out with family, friends, or just the two of us.

There was a rhythm to my life. Two holidays a year with Errol, days out, spa weekends and shopping with my girlfriends, some of whom I have known more than forty years. My grandchildren came round regularly and most weekends were spent with the family, either at my children's homes or ours. Errol kept in touch with his friends, Laurie, Tosh, Danny. He was still working away but I was accustomed to this and had created a life for myself and was reasonably content. I was looking forward to spending Christmas at my children's homes and not having to cook, just enjoying being grandma, playing with the grandchildren, and to long summer holidays with the grandchildren staying with us. I love being a grandma, my grandchildren give me lots of joy, I like being part of their lives and watching their personalities emerge. When I have a vision of the future, my grandchildren are a big part of it.

"There are many we meet who are just passing through, and then there are a few who stay to pull us through. When we reflect on who is true, it is only fitting to say thank you"

Samanthi Fernando

From a work perspective, since opening my business there have been many highlights: winning my first global contract; training the volunteers for the Commonwealth Games 2002, and appearing on the BBC local news; being the first Black female Branch Chair for Manchester CIPD; being voted one of the top 100 most influential women in the North West of England; being awarded the MBE for my contribution to business and to exporting; being head judge for the IoD, Director of the Year Awards.

I worked hard, made some sacrifices and took many risks to achieve all this, but without some wonderful clients and amazing friendships I would not have accomplished this success. When I first opened my business, someone had to take a chance on me and believe that I could make a positive impact on developing their staff. Then, as my business grew and developed, well-established organisations began to use my services. Over the years I have worked with hundreds of organisations globally, some only once but many of them in an ongoing relationship and continuing to use my services remotely after my move to the Caribbean. These organisations and my contacts within them, the CEO's, Directors, Managers, HR Specialists, Leaders, Supervisors, many of whom have become friends over the years, trusted me and drew me into their businesses and included me in their successes and celebrations. We would often meet, not just to discuss business but as friends to catch up on each other's lives over a meal and a glass of wine.

I remember having lunch with one of my contacts at an Italian restaurant. Everyone who knows me is aware of my battle with my weight and my efforts to eat healthily and on this occasion I scanned the menu and decided that a calzone, which I had eaten before at another restaurant, would be a good choice. We were catching up over a glass of wine as we waited for our food when I saw heads turning as the waiter struggled to carry the most humongous calzone I have ever seen. It could have easily fed a family of six! As the waiter put the dish down in front of me, I could see other diners looking at me in disbelief. "She's going to eat all that for her lunch!" was the unspoken comment. My companion and I stared at my plate and then at each other and burst out laughing. "So much for a light lunch!" he exclaimed.

Another wonderful memory was when a client added me to their table at an event where they had been shortlisted for an award. I was delivering management and leadership training for them, and they said they invited me because I had been part of their journey to achieving their goals. The night was a big success, as they won an award that night, but to be included in their celebration meant a lot to me.

One of my clients, a chain of international hotels, invited me to their staff award ceremony, as I had been instrumental in delivering the training for a successful initiative which considerably increased sales. Attending the event and being seen as part of the organisation's achievements made me feel loved and valued.

On many occasions when I was renting my serviced offices, I would receive a call from reception saying that a parcel had arrived for me. When I opened the box, there would be gifts from my clients. Christmas hampers, champagne, flowers, chocolates, all totally unexpected. As these clients were already paying me, I was overwhelmed that they also wanted to send gifts to me to show their appreciation.

I had built a powerful network of amazing people, who had a real interest in my success. This included being part of the Rose Review into Female Entrepreneurship. As part of my work with the NatWest Entrepreneur Accelerator, I was part of a panel sharing my views on the barriers to success for women and the event ended with lunch at Coutts in Manchester. I worked with the Department for International Trade (DIT), now called Department for Business and Trade, as an Export Champion, coaching companies who wanted to export their goods and services; there were many opportunities to give back, but also many opportunities to network, participate in events and grow and develop my international knowledge.

One of my clients, now a friend and Director of the Women of The Year Awards (WOTY), invited me to be an ambassador for this event. It was one of the best events I have ever attended, held in a beautiful venue, celebrating the achievements of some incredible women, with stimulating speakers and great networking, and I attended every year until I emigrated. I always left the event invigorated, my creative juices flowing.

Warren Buffet once said "I measure success by how many people love me!" and I am happy to say that I received a great deal of love and affection from my clients and my friends. After the ceremony at Buckingham Palace, where I was awarded my MBE, we celebrated with a beautiful family lunch at the Ritz Hotel in London. My husband, children and grandchildren were all there and I will never forget the feeling of contentment and joy. If I was to place that feeling on Maslow's Hierarchy of Needs, I would say that I felt *'self-actualization'* – which is the desire to become the most that one can be! I looked at the faces of my family and truly felt that I had reached the prime of my life - I couldn't imagine topping this achievement.

What surprised me and made me realise what strong pillars of support I had in my life, was the reaction of my genuine friends when I was awarded the MBE. Three different groups of friends arranged three separate celebration parties for me, each one complete with a cake with MBE on it! They were so pleased and proud of me. There are many more people who I would like to thank for their generosity, kindness, and support, but to do that I would have to write another book. They know who they are, and I thank you!

Past my prime?

Olive Strachan Consultancy had been established for twenty-five years, I had built a reputation and was feeling a sense of achievement.

I had contracts to deliver leadership training both in the UK and abroad, and I had established myself within the professional business community. I did feel that I was in my working prime, having achieved success in my industry. However, there were some areas in my professional life that caused me to pause for thought. I was fast approaching my late fifties and I found that when I attended conferences within the HR profession most of the people in the room seemed to be a mass of young people, mainly female, the majority in their thirties. I started to feel slightly uncomfortable at these events, there was no one who looked remotely like me. HR was supposed to represent diversity but visually this was not the impression given. With the best will in the world, it is difficult to understand the lived experience of someone who is so remote from your own personal experience. When I was working with my clients or spending time with my family and friends, I felt vital, full of energy, with plenty to contribute. Attending networking events, they all seemed geared towards younger people. Many of my more mature CIPD associates with whom I had made connections over the years, were considering retiring because of illness, or aging parents. I started to contemplate whether this was the next step for me. In a world full of bright young people all pushing forward in pursuit of achieving their goals, was I past my prime?

It's not all about me

I had achieved more in my life than expected and was happy, apart from allowing the views of society which dictate that a woman in her fifties is old and therefore invisible, to occasionally undermine my confidence. However, it was obvious that Errol was not happy. Part of the reason why he worked away was because he couldn't stand the six months or more of the year when Manchester was grey and rainy. He complained bitterly about the weather and although he loved coming home I could see that he was also looking forward to returning to his job in warmer climes.

From the first day that we met, Errol was honest with me, he said that anyone he married had to be prepared to live in the Caribbean, because that was his life's goal. During our married life, he put things in place for his dream to be realised.

We visited Jamaica frequently, perhaps eight or nine times during our marriage, hiring a car and travelling all over the island I grew to love. Errol regularly searched the internet looking for suitable properties in Jamaica. We planned to open an account with Jamaica National Bank and attended all the meetings they held in the UK for Jamaicans living abroad who wanted to invest there. Errol wanted to open a business there for future investment, and he did just that with his sister Sharon. We joined the Jamaica Society, and I joined the Leeward Island Association.

Despite all these subtle hints, I kept thinking it would happen one day but in my mind I thought it would be when we were in our seventies. When Errol started seriously discussing the move, around 2007, I must admit I wasn't ready. He started looking at property in Jamaica and even earmarked a farm he had seen as our potential home. I felt complete panic! It was a large farm in the middle of nowhere and the thought of the isolation terrified me. Thankfully, after seeing my reaction, he realised that if we were going to make this move there had to be some compromises to accommodate me. Soon after, we visited my homeland of Dominica and Errol fell completely in love with the island. We purchased some land in preparation for our retirement. I prevaricated for quite a while because I was happy with things the way they were but in 2017 Errol put his foot down. He was ready to start his new life.

As far as I was concerned, I had the life I had always envisioned. My children had their own lives, my daughter happily married with a child, my son engaged with plans to marry in the future with his family. I babysat when needed and the children came to stay with me on a regular basis, and I loved taking them for days out to the zoo, theatres, and museums. At weekends I would invite them over or I would visit them. We had no debts, I had an excellent social life, and I was enjoying my business. I really didn't want to move to the Caribbean. We discussed having a holiday home in Dominica and dividing our time between the Caribbean and the UK but as we explored all the possibilities we realised it would be impossible to keep our lovely home in the UK as well as build the house of our dreams in the Caribbean; it just wasn't viable.

Planning our Caribbean home

In 2008 we had visited Dominica with a view to locating the site for our potential holiday home. We firstly used a map and drove around various areas. The Calibishie Coast, which is located on the north-east coast of the island, is considered to be one of the most scenic and unspoiled regions of Dominica. We looked at Salisbury, located on the west coast of the island. We tried Soufriere on the south-west coast, and finally La Plaine, where my parents lived. They are all stunning locations with lots to offer but in the end we used the services of a company called Blue Sky Realtors in Roseau to help us decide. The owner, Paul Blanchard, took the details of our ideal location and suggested we look at some land not far from Roseau, on a hill overlooking the sea. My father was still alive when we bought the land and he immediately started reminiscing about his childhood; apparently he used to pick mangoes in this exact area, as a boy. When we purchased the land the area was well sought after but since then it has become even more so. It wasn't all plain sailing. We put an offer for the land but someone else had already made an offer. We were very disappointed and gave Paul our details; he now had a good picture of what we wanted and he would keep us informed. However, Errol was certain that the land would be ours and a few weeks later we received a phone call to say that the other buyer could not proceed with the sale. We sought the services of a local solicitor and we became landowners. My parents were over the moon and were looking forward to us moving to Dominica. Unfortunately, my father died of cancer in 2011 and never had the opportunity to visit us in our new home.

I resisted the move for quite a while, insisting that I was happy in the UK and that I didn't want to leave my family and friends. I know of many West Indian couples who end up separating over this issue. Usually, it's the husband who wants to return to the Caribbean and the wife does not. Often it reaches a stalemate, with the husband going to the Caribbean by himself and meeting someone else and the wife remaining in the UK. I did contemplate remaining in the UK, continuing with the life that I loved, but I couldn't imagine life without the husband I also loved. So gradually I got on board and started to help to plan our future move. Two things that made the prospect of leaving the UK more attractive were the Covid pandemic, the impact of which I have already mentioned, and Brexit.

The impact of Brexit on race relations in the UK

"Brexit" is the name given to the United Kingdom's departure from the European Union, a combination of 'Britain' and 'exit'. Boris Johnson, Prime Minister at the time, said: "On 31 January 2020 the UK left the EU. We got Brexit done to take back control, to make our own laws, and to manage our own money. The United Kingdom's uncoupling from the rules, regulations and institutions of Brussels was never simply about the moment of our departure; the act of Brexit was not an end in itself but the means by which our country will achieve great things. And so that historic night two years ago marked not the final page of the story, but the start of a whole new chapter for our country, our economy, and our people. A future in which we don't sit passively outside the European Union but seize the incredible opportunities that our freedom presents and use them to build back better than ever before making our businesses more competitive and our people more prosperous."

This rhetoric gave the impression that Brexit would bring a better life for all. However, something that was not foreseen was the increase in racism in the UK. As someone who had made the UK their home for over fifty years, the reaction by some members of society reminded me of what I faced when I first came to the UK as a young child. Suddenly, complete strangers had no compunction in shouting out racist statements to anyone who was not white. I was abused in the street and was urged to return to my own country. As someone who has lived and worked here, employed staff, and contributed to the success of the UK economy, I was extremely angry and hurt by this.

In an article in *The Guardian* dated 20 May 2019, by Robert Booth, Social Affairs Correspondent, he quoted some figures. "Survey shows 71% of people from ethnic minorities faced discrimination, up from 58%." He went on to say that "Ethnic minorities are facing rising and increasingly overt racism, with levels of discrimination and abuse continuing to grow in the wake of the Brexit referendum. Racists are feeling increasingly confident in deploying overt abuse or discrimination, with social media normalising hate and increasing division." At the same time, the BBC sacked presenter Danny Baker for tweeting a picture of a couple with a chimp, following the birth of the son of the Duke and Duchess of Sussex.

There was a definite shift in behaviour, with people who had previously hidden their racist tendencies now expressing their hate for minorities more freely, both face to face and online. It was as though we had lifted a rock and there was something nasty underneath that Brexit had released. This, together with the impact of Covid, accelerated my desire to experience a more positive environment.

CHAPTER 13
And so the adventure begins

Funding our move to Dominica

The plan was to build our Caribbean home without a mortgage. We therefore had to find the necessary cash to build our home and then fully furnish it. My husband organised an architect to bring his idea into a working model and finally we had a 3D model of our future home, including the landscaping. My husband had thought of every detail, right through to the lighting for each room and even the types of plants and fruit trees we would have in the garden. It was early 2017 and after spending some time researching building companies in Dominica, we found a company that had been established for many years and had a good reputation for the quality of their work. We travelled to Dominica, had a meeting with company and agreed that work would commence later that year. Errol and I created a plan for how we would execute this move, with each of us having a role to play in making this happen.

We had heard many horror stories from friends who had built their own homes abroad, from the house not being built to the required specifications, to inferior materials being used, or the substandard quality of workmanship. The only way to guarantee getting what you wanted or had paid for was to have a project manager on site to oversee the build. This was going to be our forever home, we had cashed in all our savings and were about to sell our house to finance this build, so we decided that I would remain in the UK and keep working whilst organising the sale of our house, and Errol would move to Dominica to be on site every day to ensure that our home was created to his exact specification.

We sprang into action and started the process, officially confirming with the building company in Dominica that we would like to go ahead. I am very organised when it comes to business but my husband even more so. Each phase of our move and the building of the house were planned in minute detail. What we hadn't planned for was hurricane Maria!

It was September 2017 and when I heard on the news that there was a hurricane heading for Dominica, I immediately called my mother to make sure she was okay and check that she was prepared for the "category 2 hurricane" heading her way. I remember her being extremely calm. This was not the first hurricane she had experienced; she had been in Dominica when hurricane David hit the island in 1979. My sisters Liza and Sharon were with her, as well as her granddaughters, Malika and Daniella, and when I spoke to her she was happily watching television. I was worried and begged her to be safe and take care, but her words to me were "Olive, when God crooks his fingers, we all cry." In other words, it was out of our hands and we must accept whatever happens, so at that point I felt fairly reassured and didn't feel there was too much cause for concern.

To keep abreast of what was happening we watched all the news updates and became increasingly anxious as we saw the hurricane change from a category 2 to a category 5. The news was of fatalities, destruction, and devastation. I was in a complete panic, not sure if my family had survived and unable to contact them as the power lines were down. Neither Errol nor I slept much that night, constantly trying to contact my family in Dominica to no avail.

Hurricane Maria had a catastrophic impact on Dominica which obviously had an impact on our plans to build a house. When we visited, not long after the hurricane, my family home had lost its roof and Mum and my sisters were all living in what used to be the bakery. All-important paperwork, clothes and family memories had been damaged by water and my mum was pretty shaken by the experience. We asked what we could do and the most immediate things they needed were food, clothes, and bedding. Luckily, many of the voluntary groups on the island had organised emergency food and clothing, but what was most noticeable as we travelled around the island was the amount of blue tarpaulin covering many of the houses as makeshift roofs. It was sad to see houses lying upside down on riverbanks, buildings with no roofs, and debris and mud everywhere. But the most poignant thing was seeing such a green and lush island as Dominica with all the trees stripped of their leaves, leaving just bare stumps of wood.

We met with our builder to see if it was still feasible to go ahead and build our home in Dominica. He explained that because the island was in such a state of devastation whoever could leave the island had gone abroad, as living in the post-hurricane conditions was extremely uncomfortable. This meant that a lot of the experienced labourers he would have used were no longer on the island. Also, there would be challenges regarding receiving shipments of materials to build the house.

After much discussion we decided that there was no timeline as to when Dominica would be back on its feet again, so we pressed ahead and confirmed that we would like to continue with the build. My husband remained in Dominica to supervise the build and I returned to the UK to get on with the house sale. I secured the services of one of the best estate agents in the area and within a few weeks of advertising our beautiful family home, with all its memories of Christmases, First Communions, children's parties, family get-togethers and VE day celebrations, was sold. Some small consolation was that the family who purchased it had two young children, so the house would continue to be a family home.

It is said that buying or selling a house is one of the most stressful experiences in life, and I can confirm that! It was compounded by the fact that I had to send all conveyancing documentation and legal documents requiring Errol's signature to Dominica by DHL couriers. It was a long and protracted process. Selling the house gave us the capital needed to fund our Caribbean home. Errol would then rent a property in Dominica whilst supervising the build and I would rent a property not too far away from the recently sold family home, meaning that I was still close to my son and his family, and my friends. It was time to take the first step in the transition process of starting a new life. Leaving the home I had known for twenty-eight years was quite a wrench, and things didn't go smoothly. Our solicitor kept asking for a date when the purchasers of our house were moving in and it kept changing weekly, so when the actual date arrived I only had an hour or so to move the rest of my furniture out of the house and hand over the key. My last memory of moving out is of the new owners driving up in a van to take possession of the house, my own removal van parked outside loaded with my furniture, ready to leave. As I was about to hand over the keys, I looked at the bay windows at the front of the house and realised that I had forgotten to take my beautiful caramel coloured velvet curtains, which my husband loved. Feeling stressed and worn out I thought I'd just leave them for the new owners, but because they were rather special, and they were a big part of memories of our first home together, I decided to go back for them. Just as the new owners were putting their furniture into the room I dashed in, grabbed the curtains by the hem and just pulled. I remember all the little white holders that attach at the top of the curtain flying out everywhere, making a pinging sound as they went! I grabbed the curtains, shoved them under my arm, climbed into the van and left for my new temporary home.

I never realised how much leaving my home would affect me. When I opened the door and stepped into my new rental home, I felt a huge sense of loss and displacement. Most of our furniture had gone into storage, but I still had about twenty-five boxes to unpack, even though the removal men had helped make me comfortable by placing everything in the right rooms. That first night in my new home I looked up at the unfamiliar ceiling and shed some tears. But there was no going back, so once again I squared my shoulders, took a deep breath, and got on with it.

My temporary home lasted for two years; I moved in there in 2018 and didn't leave until 2020. I was fortunate that there was a strong community spirit in the street, there was always some sort of get together and we had a little community garden at the end of the street. My son lived around the corner with his family so together with them and my neighbours I wasn't too lonely. Within a few weeks of moving in, a little piece of paper was put through the letterbox inviting me to a party in the garden. This happened frequently, sometimes one or two neighbours would meet, sometimes a lot more; we would all bring something to eat and drink. I spent many happy afternoons and weekends drinking, chatting and laughing whilst bonding with my new neighbours in the community garden.

The best laid plans

The house had been sold and we now had the capital necessary to start building. Errol had challenges which ranged from finding experienced labour to difficulties with the land, which had to be levelled out and a digger hired to remove rocks, etc.

As we were building our dream home, I decided that I would need a dream kitchen! I was walking around Urmston, where I was living at that time and saw a company that designed bespoke kitchens. I walked in and the salesman gave me a tour of the various kitchens available. I walked around the store visualising myself in my beautiful kitchen, with sleek appliances, reverently running my hands over the smooth granite worktops. I was given some brochures to take home so that I could select the combination that was right for me. After a week of poring over the brochure, I made my decision and returned to the store. I wanted to make sure that my kitchen was paid for in advance so there would be no possibility of us running out of funds. I worked with the kitchen designer along with input from Errol, as he had designed the house and kitchen area, so it was designed to the exact specification. I spent many hours just looking at my kitchen in 3D, imagining it installed into my Caribbean home.

When the time approached for us to fill our container bound for Dominica with all our worldly goods, I went to the kitchen supplier and requested that they organise for my kitchen to be shipped to our removal company. I had a few moments of concern when the salesman who had sold me the kitchen started making excuses as to why they couldn't expedite this immediately. He said there would be some delay as there were issues with one of their suppliers, and he then asked me if I had paid for my kitchen on my credit card because if there was a problem, I could claim the cost of my kitchen back. Alarm bells started ringing in my head and I had a sinking feeling in my stomach. I called the company every day and each time I was informed that they were just waiting for one of my cupboards and to be patient. I visited my husband in Dominica in July 2020 and when I returned I visited the premises of the company in question. To my dismay all I could see was mail piled up at the letterbox and no staff in the shop. The company had gone bankrupt, and I had lost all my money. It was a scandal in the area at the time, with many other unfortunate people being left out of pocket for a kitchen they would never receive. I was devastated and felt very anxious about telling Errol about this blow. He already had enough problems that come with building a house, he just didn't need this as well. I took the coward's way out and kept putting it off until one day, when Errol was visiting me, he passed the shop in Urmston and it was obvious it was no longer trading. He came home looking completely shocked and I had to explain what had happened, showing him the letters from the receivers clarifying that the company had gone into receivership and that we were on a long list of creditors. It was a big blow and he was understandably angry and frustrated by the situation we were in but in the end he was pragmatic about it. This had been my dream bespoke kitchen, it was extremely costly and I knew that I wouldn't be able to amass the amount of revenue required to purchase anything like this again, so I had to compromise and buy a more cost-effective version.

We faced many challenges before we finally left the UK and the experience made me more resilient. It is good to plan but sometimes your plans go awry and you just have to deal with it and carry on.

CHAPTER 14
Making the transition

When shifts and
Transitions in life shake
You to the core, see that
As a sign of the greatness
That's about to occur.

Drew Adelman, PhD

Making the transition

I can truthfully say that leaving the UK after living there for fifty-three years of my life, from 1967 to 2020, shook me to the core. At the beginning of the Covid pandemic Errol was living and working in Dublin, Ireland, and I was living in Urmston. As an extrovert who gains energy, joy, and purpose from my interaction with people, not being able to go out of the house and meet people was something that I had never experienced before and found difficult to deal with. I did receive support from family and friends but life just wasn't the same. I can understand why there are reports on the long-term mental health problems suffered by young people because of the Covid pandemic. I am an adult with a great deal of life experience and some days when I looked at the four walls and listened to the news report on how many people in the UK had contracted Covid that day, and how many had died, I would feel a sense of panic and doom. I can't begin to contemplate how parents of young children coped, or young people who couldn't go out and meet friends.

Eventually it became clear that Covid was not going to be over in a month, as we all assumed when it began. This was a long-term serious issue, impacting on the global population. Errol came home from Ireland and joined me in Urmston. Although the house in Dominica wasn't completely ready, we knew that we could live there and gradually complete the necessary work. When Errol arrived back in Manchester we completed last minute arrangements, giving notice to utility companies etc, ready to leave.

We booked our flights through our lovely travel agent, Daryl Glean at Travel Counsellors. Because of Covid the paperwork seemed never ending, with every airport we were to pass through, even in transit, needing documentation. We had Covid tests which proved negative, but we then had to be very careful about having contact with anyone just before flying, so when the removal men arrived we made sure all the windows and doors were open and wore our masks. We kept ourselves as isolated as possible, worried that if we tested positive it would mean losing our flights. We also had a forty-foot container on its way to Dominica, and we needed to be there to accept delivery. There was a lot riding on this.

Under normal circumstances we would have had a leaving party to say goodbye to family and friends but because of the pandemic my friends resorted to sending cards and flowers to my house; some even came and stood in the road outside my house to say goodbye on the day we left. My son and grandchildren stood in the street and the grandchildren waved, desperate to hug us goodbye but not allowed. My neighbours made a Dominican flag and congregated outside the house to give us a send-off. It was so sad. I am a tactile person and it was very hard not to hug everyone. On the way to London we stopped off at Wolverhampton to say goodbye to my daughter and her family, and once again I was devastated that I couldn't hug my granddaughter, only wave goodbye from a distance.

As we drove to the airport a kaleidoscope of memories flashed before my eyes: arriving in the UK for the first time; singing at the school play at primary school with my parents in the audience; Dad taking us to see Johnny Nash at Romeo and Juliette's night club in Blackburn when I was eleven years old; getting married and walking down the aisle in my wedding dress and Dad giving me away; giving birth to my children; moving into our first home; opening my own business; winning my first contract; my daughter's wedding; the births of my four grandchildren; celebrating my husband's sixtieth birthday at Centre Parcs with the whole family; going to Buckingham Palace to accept my MBE. On and on, the memories flooded my mind making me feel desperately sad.

In the UK, I didn't always win the game, but I knew the rules of the game and how to play. In Dominica I felt like I was going into the unknown. The benefits were that my mother and sisters were there. One of the downsides was that during my visits there I was often too hot and I have the type of skin that gets bitten by every bug going. I loved visiting Dominica and Jamaica on holiday but after two weeks I was always glad to get back to my cool sheets and no mosquito bites. I do love looking at beautiful scenery but unlike my husband, who just loves looking at green, lush landscapes, I can take it or leave it. In the UK when we had the overcast and rainy days which are prevalent in Manchester my husband would hate it, whereas it didn't bother me at all. I would prefer to be cool rather than hot and to me where there is heat and greenery there are bugs which bite! In all honesty I must confess that I am a city girl at heart - give me the skyscrapers, shops, cinemas, and theatres, I love it all! Leaving made me feel like I was giving up everything I was comfortable and familiar with, whereas Errol couldn't wait to go! After all, he had instigated the move, had already spent a lot of time in Dominica, and was generally much happier and ready to take the final step.

We arrived at the airport in London, which was practically deserted due to Covid, and the plane was only a third full. We had to wear masks for the whole journey apart from when we were eating. It was a nine-hour flight but we were anxious and unable to relax as we knew that on arrival we would have to test again and if we did test positive for Covid it would cause complications.

Out of my comfort zone

We arrived in Dominica on 11 October 2020 and were ushered to a section of Douglas Charles airport specifically reserved for international travellers to be tested for Covid. The staff who checked us were in full protective gear, it wasn't a pleasant experience, and once again we sat anxiously waiting for the results of our tests. Finally, we received the all clear and were picked up by our Covid certified driver and taken to our Covid certified accommodation. We stayed at Rose Street Gardens, Goodwill, a suburb of the capital, Roseau. Our host was Jennifer Fadelle. We had to follow strict Covid protocol, which involved taking our temperatures and recording them daily. We were not allowed to leave but thankfully it's a lovely guest house overlooking Roseau and we spent many hours sitting in the beautiful garden. Jennifer was the perfect host; she is also an event planner and caterer so was able to organise some delicious meals to be delivered to us. I must admit that after a week of not going out and eating some marvellous food, my jeans were hard to fasten!

After the prerequisite quarantine period we were allowed to complete our quarantine at our new home. Jennifer very kindly drove us and allowed us to borrow a basket full of plates and cutlery. I have remained in contact with Jennifer to this day, I love reading her posts on Facebook which are informative and funny! Our house was built and had a roof but it still needed work and we had no furniture, as everything we had was on the container ship making its way to Dominica. My sister organised delivery of a bed for us and my mum gave us a sofa, table, plates, pots, and pans.

Errol and I had spent seven months incarcerated in our home in the UK. When Covid first came to light in March 2020 we were given the impression that it was a short-term problem. We were told that if we remained in our home, kept isolated, and wore our masks when we went out things would get better. Instead, we lived in some sort of dystopian hell, of constant news about how many people had died of Covid that day, how many new cases of Covid had been recorded, and pictures of people gasping for breath and at death's door in the hospital wards. It was difficult not to get depressed and although I was sad to leave my family and friends it felt like heaven to arrive at our Caribbean home. We still had to remain isolated but my family had left us some groceries and together with some supplies from Jennifer we had enough food. My husband had ensured that we had running water and electricity and whilst we were in the UK Liza and her friend Ozzie had planted the garden with plants and shrubs to Errol's specific design. We have almost half an acre of land surrounding the house and it was absolute bliss to be able to sit in the garden, look at the flowers, breathe fresh air and enjoy the space and freedom of our own property.

Gradually some of the gnawing anxiety I had been feeling began to lift and the sun made me feel a sense of optimism. There were flowers blooming everywhere. Although the house was really not quite ready to move into, we decided that rather than pay rent we would live there, albeit it was a little basic. The money saved would go towards buying essential supplies, such as cement, bricks, paint, etc. Saying you don't mind a few months of being uncomfortable whilst the house is finished off is easy, actually living somewhere without all your creature comforts is something else entirely, as I was soon to find out!

Dominica has a tropical climate and the centipedes, crickets, lizards, and tiny frogs, none of which I was accustomed to, had taken up residence in our absence. My husband took it all in his stride, whilst I spent a lot of the time shrieking as tiny insects went about their everyday business. When I look back on those early days of my adjustment to living in a tropical climate I think of Maslow's hierarchy of needs. It starts with physiological needs, which include sleep, warmth etc. I was sleeping poorly because I had lived for most of my life in a climate that ranged from -3°C to 20°C. There are exceptions but in England the weather is generally cool, summers tend to be brief with quite a bit of rain, and I was happy with the temperature, only suffering during unusually cold winters. In Dominica I would look at the night-time temperature on my phone and it would say 26°C. The mosquitoes love me and unless I put on some kind of repellent I have lumps and bumps all over my skin in no time. We had running water in our new house but no shower had yet been installed, so Errol rigged up the garden hose, which he fed through the window of the outside washroom, put the hose in the heat to get warm and hey presto! Turn on the tap and you could have a warm shower!

One of our first tasks was to engage the services of a company that could help us complete our home to a comfortable standard. It is always good to ask for recommendations and we were given the name of a building company by two different people. Errol sent out his specification, we received a quote and before long we had approximately six men working under Errol's direction to turn our house into the home we dreamed of. Our house is designed in two stories. Downstairs there is an apartment which is self-contained. Our plan is to rent the apartment out for two reasons. One is that it's always good to have more than one source of income, and secondly we hope to have guests from all over the world which, as we get older, will be a great way of meeting new people. Upstairs we have our own luxury apartment. It is very beautiful and spacious, with large windows, each one framing a different part of the garden and landscape. From one window we can see the mountains in the distance, from another we can watch the sunset over the sea, and from another all you can see is foliage and greenery, truly a feast for the eyes and senses. We have an assortment of furniture, some pieces we have had for years, and we purchased a few new ones. When we have Zoom calls with our children in the UK, they say it looks and feels like home, because of all the family pictures and familiar objects we have dotted around.

Prior to Hurricane Maria, Dominica's rental market was booming and hopefully it will again. Errol is very capable and completed some of the work himself, tiling, painting, and installing both kitchens in the house, amongst other things. In our previous home in the UK, he installed the central heating himself and completed most repairs on the house. In the Caribbean we use outside labour when we need to but Errol is very capable and I am very fortunate to have him. It's a large house so work is still ongoing, however, I live in a beautiful, comfortable home.

Our first year living in Dominica was all about working on the house and Errol was extremely busy, advising the builders or working on some projects himself. I unfortunately, have no such skills. My father was the person in our house who put plugs on or did any DIY around the home, and I must admit I had no desire to start at this stage of my life. My day consisted of getting up, making cups of tea, and cooking meals, washing up, and cleaning. In my previous life I was involved in the corporate life, running my own business and loving it! I quickly became very bored and felt that my life had no purpose. When I returned to Dominica, I was fifty-nine years old and had considered semi retiring, but within a month I knew that it was not for me!

Having lived in the UK for so long I had a group of friends that I could rely on. Friends from university, work colleagues and many of my clients that I had worked for over the years had also become friends. Errol had never had a strong desire to go out or socialise much, but I had! If I wanted to go to the theatre, the cinema, lunch, or a meal, a day of shopping, a visit to London, I had a girl friend I could call on to share the experience with. I also had my children and grandchildren; they obviously had their own families, but I was part of their family and they would include me. We would go for trips out, take the grandchildren to various activities, and my diary was always full of fun things to do. In Dominica, I had my mum and sisters in La Plaine and I enjoyed visiting them, but they had their own lives. Fortunately, we had purchased a car, although I was nervous about driving in Dominica because of the hilly terrain with lots of windy roads, some of them still crumbling and difficult to navigate post-hurricane. After driving my husband mad with my constant complaints about how lonely I was and how much I missed my children and grandchildren he was relieved when I would go out for the day, leaving him in peace to focus on completing the house. Often, I would call him if I was delayed in traffic and he would say "No need to rush back, see you when I see you!" Most days after breakfast, I would jump into the car and just drive, anywhere.

My sister Liza is well known in Dominica. She used to work at a hair salon called *Caprice* which was one of the best known in Dominica and where lots of businesspeople and radio presenters etc went to have their hair styled, and consequently she has many connections. Liza is also an entrepreneur: she is still a professional stylist and has some core clients, but she also has a grocery shop, and sells nearly new clothing as well. Dominica is a small island with not a lot of footfall so most people have a "side hustle". Even people in full time employment do this to bring in extra income.

In those early months I spent most of my time just wandering around Roseau having lunch alone and feeling very sorry for myself until one day I was sitting in a restaurant called Petit Paris, staring at the sea despondently, when my daughter rang to see how I was. I was feeling dejected and described how bored I was and that I longed to return to the UK to all that was familiar. My daughter said "Mum, you love the world of business, find out where the centre of business is in Dominica and join." My son also contacted me and said the exact same thing "You love the business world, just do what you love."

Don't put the key to your happiness in someone else's pocket!

After this pep talk from my children, I realised that I was looking to my husband to make me happy. As someone who loves quotes and mantras, I read the above quote and realised that I couldn't put the burden for making me happy on my husband's shoulders. It was down to me to find the key to my own happiness. As I said earlier, I love the world of business and when I hit a brick wall I tend to look at how I can apply business solutions to a personal life problem. I decided to complete a Gap Analysis on my life in Dominica. I looked at my current state and I looked at my desired state, I then listed the key steps to bridge the gap and completed an action plan.

The situation was that I had no real purpose in my life. Waking up, cleaning the house and cooking just didn't motivate or excite me! I had been thinking about semi retiring, this experience made it clear that I was just not ready. I took to lying in bed as long as possible to make the day go faster, because when I woke up there would be about six men working on the house. It was a very male environment and Errol was in his element. After I had made the prerequisite teas and coffees, I was just in the way and could see the relief on their faces when I jumped into the car and drove off to have an adventure.

My current state was bored, frustrated, feeling completely out of my depth. I started off by looking at my contacts, who did I know in Dominica? Who could give me a foot into the door of Dominican life? On a previous visit to Dominica, my sister Liza had introduced me to her friend Cecily Lees, who in turn had invited me to her *Ladies Night Out* network. The person who had established the group was Tina Alexander, and since joining the network in 2018 I had kept in touch via Facebook.

My plan of action began! I contacted Tina and Marieke Van Asten, who I had also met at the network, and we arranged to meet for lunch. It was lovely just to sit and chat. They were also really helpful with advice regarding finding doctors, dentists, and potential contacts. I came home energised and started to construct a list of contacts that could prove useful in Dominica. Cecily and her husband Colin had really looked after Errol during the time he lived in Dominica on his own, whilst he supervised the building of our home. When I first arrived we did not immediately get together because of Covid restrictions, however, we did meet out in the open at Mero beach which is near their home, for lunch and a swim in the sea, which was lovely. Both Tina and Cecily have lived in Dominica for over twenty-five years and in that time they have established businesses, purchased land, constructed homes. Between them they have contacts at all levels of society in Dominica and they have been invaluable in helping me to not only make the right contacts but to integrate.

Tina invited me to the next *Ladies Night Out* networking group, it was just what I needed socially. The group is quite big, with over forty members, with a range of ages and professions. Everyone stays connected via a WhatsApp group and there is a lot of support for one other. We either find new up and coming restaurants to visit or we all bring some food and visit someone's house. If we are going for a night out and we want to have a drink, we sometimes hire a minibus which picks us up and drops us back at our door. There is a lot of laughter, good food and good company. This is a great network for socialising, it got me out of the house and allowed me to meet people. On my second outing with the group we visited a beautiful bed and breakfast called Charlotte Estate, an amazing old house built in the 1920's, named after Queen Charlotte, wife of King George III. The manicured gardens are fabulous. It is run by Celine and Marcel who also own the Petit Paris restaurant. That night Tina encouraged me to deliver a short presentation about myself and to discuss my book, *The Power of You*, and consequently thirteen women from the group purchased a copy of my book to demonstrate their support, which I really appreciated. I am still a member of the group and continue to enjoy their company and attend events.

I knew that I was not happy with my life in Dominica but I had to be realistic. It had taken me many years to gain respect in the UK, establishing my own training consultancy and taking it global; being a member of the CIPD for over twenty years, including being Branch Chair; qualifying in Human Resources, with both a Post Graduate Diploma and then a Master's degree; joining the NatWest bank accelerator hub for entrepreneurs and providing coaching; being a Member of the Institute of Directors (IoD) and becoming the head judge. It had taken many years of hard work and persistence.

During Covid I had not worked a great deal, because the majority of my work was traditionally face to face. I had to develop new skills of facilitating, learning, coaching and mentoring on Zoom or Microsoft Teams. I had clients in the UK and America who I worked with remotely, but I was an unknown in Dominica and had to find a way to build my brand.

I knew that although I was Dominican by birth, to my countrymen I was seen as being English and not one of them at all. I was going to have to work hard to win their trust and prove myself before I could achieve my goal of establishing my training consultancy in the Caribbean.

CHAPTER 15
Reverse culture shock

Described as "the common reaction to returning home after being abroad", this is not a phrase that I have used before. Reverse culture shock is an emotional and psychological stage of readjustment, similar to your initial reaction when moving abroad. I had recently completed a presentation on diversity and inclusion, my own personal story, via Zoom for Liverpool University students. Afterwards I was talking to Dr Jenny Johnson, who had requested that I speak, and I was telling her how much I had struggled when I first arrived in Dominica and how challenging I found it to just fit in. She then informed me that 'reverse culture shock' was what I was experiencing and I realised that it described exactly the process that I was going through. This experience is a phenomenon that the International Organization for Migration recognises and they have a written a Reintegration Handbook about the challenges it poses.

My parents had instilled in us at an early age that our home was Dominica. Typically, they also sent money home to their family in Dominica and they always dreamed of returning to the land of their birth. My father had attempted to return to Dominica on more than one occasion. In 1972, when I was eleven years old, my parents packed up everything and we moved back to Dominica. My father, the serial entrepreneur, opened a shop in Case O' Gowrie and I remember occasionally serving in the shop. Liza and I tried our best to fit in with the other children, but even then it was a challenge because the rest of the children had shared experiences and had grown up together, whilst we were strangers. After a year, my father decided that there were more opportunities in the UK for his children and so we returned to the UK in 1973.

In 1978 my parents tried again to fulfil their dream of returning to Dominica but on this occasion my father planned it differently. My mum returned to Dominica with my two younger sisters whilst my father continued working to earn money to send to her so that she could build a home. I was in the process of taking my GCSE's so I remained in the UK with my father, whilst my sister Liza had left home to share a flat with friends. I was sixteen years old and wanted to go out with my friends and have fun, whilst my father naturally wanted me to knuckle down to my studies. I decided to leave home and moved in with my sister. My mum always said that if she had been there with me during this crucial time in my life, I would not have left home at such a young age.

Meanwhile in Dominica my mother was building a home for the family so that my father could join her. However, this was not meant to be. On 29 August 1979 Hurricane David hit the island. It was a Category 5 hurricane with winds of a hundred and fifty miles per hour and carrying millions of gallons of rain. A report on Wikipedia says that after pounding Dominica for more than six hours, seventy-five percent of the agricultural industry was destroyed, fifty-six people were dead with a further one hundred and eighty injured, and seventy five percent of the population were left homeless. For many months after the hurricane people lodged in tents or with more fortunate friends. My mum understandably wanted to return to the UK as living conditions were not favourable to say the least. My father wanted her to stay because our property had been damaged and he wanted her to wait to for some kind of compensation, ensuring that all he had invested was not lost, however, Mum insisted and back to the UK she went. My parents' dream of moving back to Dominica finally came to fruition in 1986, when I was twenty-five years old. They moved to Dominica and opened a bakery, affectionately known in the area as Bo Peep's bakery! It was a tremendous success; it grew to offer a delivery service and my parents had staff working for them to deliver the bread to different parts of the island. To this day when I mention the bakery, people exclaim about how lovely my parents' bread was and how sorry they are that it had to close.

The reason for closure was down to a congenital eye problem in my family which seems to affect the males. My father went blind before he died, as did his father before him. When he had lost sight in one eye and his sight was diminishing in the other, Errol and I arranged for my father to see a specialist in the UK. The specialist informed us that he had completed some research into this form of blindness, where certain villages had this problem. Sadly, the blood vessels had burst at the back of my father's eyes, killing the nerves, and the same was happening to his other eye. Maybe if he had come sooner they could have saved his sight, but it was too late. Following this prognosis, I always make sure I share this information with the ophthalmologist when I have my eyes tested, in order to check for any signs of this problem. My parents' dream became a reality; they had returned home, opened a successful business and established themselves, but due to Dad's blindness the bakery had to close. After this final trip to see the specialist, my father never again returned to the UK before he died in 2011, and my mother also remained in Dominica until her death in 2021.

Reading about my parents' three attempts to return to their homeland one can see how our heritage, and the fact that we had a home in Dominica, was instilled in us at an early age, so it was a shock to realise when you actually get there that you are not seen as Dominican. The paradox is that you were seen as a foreigner in the UK and are now seen as a foreigner in the country of your birth. But like most things in life, you have to work hard to achieve your goal and it takes time. To combat the feeling of isolation that I felt early on, I researched different experiences of friends and contacts about how they had integrated into a new country. My friend Candace Edwards had left the UK to live in Malaga, Spain, and a key thing for her was to learn the language before making the move, because being able to communicate is vital. Candace had also lived in Australia for two years, in the 1980's, and explained how it had taken many months to find her feet, make friends and begin to feel settled. I also spoke to Louise Duncan from TetraMap© who had moved from the UK to New Zealand; she shared the fact that the first two years were challenging. I then spoke to returnees in Dominica, my sister Liza amongst others, and the story was the same - the first few years were a difficult period of adjustment.

The psychosocial challenges of being a returnee

It is reassuring to know that my experience of being a returnee is not just something that I have experienced but it happens globally. In a paper called "Coming home can be harder than leaving" by the International Organization for Migration (IOM) it examines the reintegration process of migrants and defines it as "the incorporation of a person into a group or process that enables the returnee to participate again in the social, cultural, economic and political life of his or her country of origin." The report goes on to say that reintegration is all wrapped up with identity. There are four aspects: (1) how you are perceived by others; (2) roles and social expectations; (3) culture and traditions, and (4) how a person views themselves as an individual.

Returnees experience these challenges to their identity not only during transit and upon arrival at their destination, but also during the process of returning and re-adapting to their communities of origin.

The reintegration process depends on how long you spent abroad, in my case fifty-three years, and the extent to which you kept in contact with friends and family whilst you were away. In my case, because I left as a young child, I had no friends to keep in contact with. As an adult I visited my Mum and Dad in Dominica, but this was for two weeks at a time. A visit to extended family for an hour or so does not create a long term and lasting relationship.

Learning to adapt, and juggling with transnational identities makes it difficult for returning migrants to fit in to their community of origin. This can lead to social exclusion which is a risk to the emotional well-being of returning migrants, which in turn can have negative psychological consequences such as depression and anxiety. Reading this factual report on what it is like to be a migrant and the difficulty of integration made me curious to dig deeper into this subject. A short story called *Madame Poverty* from the book *Montage Dominik, New Stories and Poems of Dominica*, written by Kristine Simelda, describes the sad story of a returnee who comes back home believing that she would be welcomed back by her childhood friends, only to find that she is on the outside looking in. Her neighbours' comment behind her back "All that time she gone, we never heard a peep. What she want with us now?" She is rich financially, but poor when it comes to friends and her community.

Gary Younge of *The Guardian* newspaper wrote an article in November 2009 called *Homeward bound: Caribbean returnees*, in which he interviewed returnees from different islands in the Caribbean, including Dominica. Eustace Maxim lives in an area called Jimmit, Dominica, and he described the panoramic view of the Caribbean Sea from his veranda. Eustace reflected that if he had retired in Plaistow, East London, he would just be sitting at home watching TV. He left Dominica in 1960 and came back in 2004; returning was always his dream. He said "There is a freedom I feel here. I have the hot sunshine on my back and can have a dip in the river or the hot springs." Although some in Dominica brand him an outsider, he shrugs and ignores the comments. "People say this, people say that."

Further in the article, Younge describes a discussion with the then Minister for Trade, Industry and Consumer and Diaspora Affairs. Regarding returnees he says "This is not the Dominica they left. Local people are not against them, they just don't know them." And a telling comment, describing the current economic situation "When the returnees left, England was on the rise, but over the last few years people are going to Venezuela, Cuba and China for education and opportunities, not England." This is evidenced by the large investment by China in Dominica, in projects such as the Windsor Park Cricket Stadium, Roseau Grammar School and the Dominica China Friendship Hospital.

Reading these articles, I wish I had completed more research before emigrating; now everything that I have experienced makes perfect sense. If I had known what to expect, the impact would have been less because I would be prepared for it. My advice for anyone considering migrating would be to research thoroughly. However, I do feel that overall this experience has increased my resilience.

Friendship and migration

Harriet Westcott, in her article on this subject dated October 2017, examines friendship in the context of migration. This is a subject close to my heart because I have suffered a lot of angst over this balancing act, keeping friends in the UK and making friends in Dominica. I have experienced challenges with both. Living in the Caribbean and having visited the UK twice in three years means that I have been able to see some of my friends but actually maintaining friendships across time zones can be problematic. What I have also found surprising is that the friends that I saw and spoke to most frequently in the UK are not the ones who have the staying power to maintain the friendship. To some, out of sight is out of mind. One friend is angry at me for leaving and although I tried to continue the friendship, I eventually had to respect that person's wishes. If they do not feel the need to keep in contact, allow them that distance. Some friendships are for a reason and a season and you have to let it go. For the friends who have kept in touch, there are a lot of shared experiences via Facebook, the birth of a baby, birthdays, anniversaries, etc. I love reading about what my friends are doing and send messages of encouragement. For friends who need a deeper conversation WhatsApp is great. My friend Marlene and I talk regularly via WhatsApp, giggling helplessly as we share anecdotes. Speaking to old friends is like climbing into a warm bath, familiar, comfortable, safe, and enjoyable.

In her article, Harriet Wescott comments "The initial period immediately following migration can be socially empty and lonely. Friendship is reciprocal, so wanting to be friends isn't enough to have a friendship, because the other person has to be interested in pursuing that too." It is easier to make friends with other migrants because we have a shared experience. We are both outsiders in a new country where we are trying to fit in and if you have migrated from the same country there are similarities, such as programmes we have seen on TV, food that we liked to eat, the English weather! In her interviews with migrants, they expressed the desire to be friends with local people, after all, having migrated to start a new life there is the desire to immerse themselves in the culture. However, migrants are in an unequal position to locals who already have an established social life, so their need for friendship is usually less pressing.

With the above insight, it became clear that keeping my old friends and making new ones was going to be hard, but I decided I would do my best to ensure that I didn't neglect my friends in the UK, and was culturally sensitive to the barriers to making new friends in Dominica. The bottom line is, I am a strong, confident, mature woman. I am not a needy person and yes, I do want to make friends, but not if it means losing my sense of self or having to be something that I am not. I have, as they say, "put myself out there" in order to meet people and enjoy the company of others.

Creating opportunities

Ladies Network Group

Prior to coming to live permanently in Dominica, my sister had introduced me to her friend Cecily, who had asked me to join her at one of her Ladies' Network Group meetings. It was held at the house of Tina Alexander, who was responsible for setting up the group originally. It was a lovely evening; we all brought some food or wine and just enjoyed one another's company. When I returned as a permanent resident, I already had three contacts from the group with whom I had kept in touch. We met for lunch and I was invited to the next meeting. The group had expanded considerably and one of its purposes was to promote new local restaurants. The group was now forty strong and we frequently booked out a whole restaurant when everyone wanted to attend. We also had our own resident poet, Jermainia Colaire-Didier, my cousin. At my first meeting, held at The Charlotte Estate in Newtown, I was given the opportunity to promote my book and perform a short presentation. This network has been instrumental in building a social life in Dominica, encouraging me to travel to different parts of the island and make connections that I would not normally have made.

Dealing with Rejection

One my main principles when coaching entrepreneurs is that they have to build and promote their brand. Visibility is the key to creating brand awareness and I knew that I needed to be more visible in Dominica within the business community. I had brought a few copies of my book, *The Power of You,* to Dominica and my thoughts were that as people read my book it would build awareness of my capabilities. There is one main, independent bookstore in Roseau called Jays Book Store. I wanted someone to facilitate a connection and I contacted my friend, Marquita, who has a career in publishing. She gave me the direct line for her contact, I called him and requested a meeting. My husband gave me a lift into Roseau and I went up the stairs to his office. I introduced myself and gave my sales pitch, giving him a copy of the book. His face remained totally impassive throughout and after I had stopped talking, he said that he would not stock my book in his store. He said he understood what the Dominican public liked to read and he didn't feel that it would sell well. I talked about my twenty-five, five-star reviews on Amazon to no avail. He was not interested full stop!

I climbed into the car with my shoulders slumped, I wanted the book to be in the local bookstore for professional but also personal reasons - my parents would have been so proud to see my book there. But it was not meant to be. My husband was very supportive and comforting. It was disappointing - but not insurmountable! After living in Dominica for a year and becoming more established within the business community, I approached the owner of the bookstore again. This time I was armed with some positive feedback from Dominicans who had read my book and found it worthwhile. I am happy to say that my book is now stocked at Jays Book Store in Roseau. It gives me immense satisfaction and pride to have my book available in the country of my birth.

My book launch at Charlotte Estate

I made the decision to have a book launch, thus giving me the opportunity to spread knowledge about my capabilities and network. I had previously visited Charlotte Estate, it has beautiful traditional West Indian architectural features such as a deep veranda, high ceilings for ventilation, wooden hurricane shutters and a steep, pitched roof, and I was impressed by how beautiful it was inside, as well as the extensive gardens outside. I liaised with Celine and Marcel who ran Charlotte Estate as a bed and breakfast venue and booked a date for the event. Most of the marketing was by social media. I have a presence on Twitter, Facebook, Instagram, and LinkedIn. I also had some leaflets printed which were distributed to local restaurants and shops. Liza used her contact list and we physically walked around Roseau selling tickets, which helped towards the cost of the event. In the end approximately twenty-two local businesses and contacts came along, together with my sister, and Ron Green and his wife Jocelyn, who were friends of my father. They came to support me as they knew how proud my father would have been if he was still with us. It was wonderful of them to take the time. The evening surpassed my expectations and whilst I was waiting to greet my guests the extrovert in me was doing mental cartwheels with excitement! As everyone arrived and the noise level lifted as they greeted each other and began to network, I felt a sense of achievement and happiness. This was just the beginning. The evening ended with me giving a short motivational speech about my entrepreneurial journey and I received great feedback. I felt invigorated by the event. I was definitely making headway with my action plan to fill the gap in my life in Dominica!

Whilst promoting my book I met the owners of the Pagua Bay House Hotel, located in Marigot, Dominica. I had passed it on numerous occasions on my way to the airport. They were disappointed that they couldn't attend my original book launch and asked that I run the event again, but this time at their hotel. The audience on this occasion were hoteliers and this was an opportunity to meet a different group of entrepreneurs. We had a delightful lunch, then I delivered a presentation. It was a good social event, and I made some new contacts. In the past I have delivered training for the hotel and travel industry, including the TUI group and Thompson Holidays. In the normal scheme of things this event would have secured some work, however, we were still in the midst of the Covid pandemic. Most of the hotels in Dominica had been hit by tropical storm Erica and then soon after, hurricane Maria. Most of them were operating with only one third occupancy, if that. The last thing on their minds was investing in training. After both events I followed up via email, making contact and requesting one-to-one meetings, but neither of these events resulted in me securing any work.

Filming my videos

My book launches had not had the desired outcome and I had to find another way of building my brand. Having worked for myself for over twenty years I had used the services of four different marketing companies which have given me some knowledge of how to use social media effectively. I posted regularly on different platforms but had only tried video on two occasions. I was at home one Saturday, mopping the floor, when I had a flash of inspiration. I would film a brief video which I would put on social media!

I researched how long a video needed to be in order to be published on social media. One minute seemed to be the optimum, with less for Twitter, and I sat down and wrote a brief speech for my first video. I quickly jumped into the shower, put on a nice dress and some makeup, and ran outside to my husband in the garden, brandishing my iPhone. "Will you help me to film a video for my social media platform?" I asked, breathless with excitement. Errol just shrugged, said okay, and washed his hands. Our garden is lovely, with lots of plants, flowers, and bird song. I stood in the garden and recited my sixty second video. We filmed a few versions until I was happy and then I sat down and uploaded my video to LinkedIn. I was honest with my audience and said that it was not professionally filmed, I was trying something new and would welcome any feedback. The engagement was high, with a lot of honest feedback and advice about how to minimise the background noise such as cars approaching and the birdsong. But everyone agreed that it was a good concept.

In total I filmed seven videos, the first one with Errol and thereafter I had friends help me, as well as a young man called Jireh, for a time, who was recommended by Kairi FM. The purpose of the film was to build my brand in the Caribbean, at the same time keeping my international clients informed of my progress with my Caribbean office. I decided that I would create a short film, each giving hints and tips to entrepreneurs from the lessons I had learnt from running a business for twenty-five years. To make the film have more impact, each video would be filmed at a different beauty spot in Dominica so that the video would not only be informative but visually pleasing too. It was important to get the right lighting, so best to film early in the morning before the sun got too high and too hot, and as many of the locations were local beauty spots we had to deal with constant interruptions from visiting sightseers! It took a lot of patience to complete the filming but it was worth it.

The first video was an introduction to me and my business and was filmed at my home. In the second we discovered how to know your strengths and weaknesses as an entrepreneur, doing a personal SWOT analysis. This was filmed at the market, giving a taste of the sights and sounds of Roseau. The third video looked at how to overcome Imposter Syndrome and was filmed at Mero beach, with the Caribbean Sea twinkling behind me, and in the fourth video I focused on how to survive a recession and we filmed it at Trafalgar Falls. The fifth video discussed insights into having a good social media presence and was filmed at Scott's Head, and the sixth gave hints and tips on networking for business success, filmed at the Emerald Pool. The final video was filmed at my home in Dominica, where I talked about leaving a legacy.

Kairi FM/Going Global

At one of the networking events held by Dominica Chamber of Commerce, I met a Dominican businesswoman who introduced me to her contact at Kairi FM radio. As a result of this, I paid for an hour's slot on the radio. Prior to going on the radio we planned our strategy and I listed the questions that I would like her to ask me in order to draw out the key messages I wanted to share, such as the fact that I was Dominican and had a rich legacy; my expertise in leadership and

HR; my business knowledge and global expertise; awards and accolades won; what I could offer to Dominicans; and, last but not least, my availability for work. Although this interview did not produce immediate outcomes, it laid some of the foundations for my future success.

The seven short videos were a catalyst for achieving some positive outcomes in my search for securing some work. Firstly, I sent my videos out to contacts in Dominica via WhatsApp. Steve Vidal from Kairi saw one of my short videos, filmed at Mero beach, and he was impressed. He suggested that I come into Kairi FM offices and meet the station manager as they had an idea for me. They suggested that I have a morning slot on the radio, 7.55am, drive time. The programme would be called "Going Global" and I would have eight slots aligned to my short videos, each slot lasting for approximately five minutes, and I would share hints and tips about how to take your business global. It was quite exciting and for me a whole new way of marketing myself, even though initially it took me out of my comfort zone. This definitely increased my brand awareness as suddenly I started to get phone calls from people who had listened to me broadcasting.

The second positive thing to happen was that my friend Cecily Lees also saw one of my videos and was impressed. She contacted one of her business connections in Dominica and recommended my services. This resulted in a meeting and although the organisation didn't book my services straight away, it converted into some leadership training work the following year.

My Cheerleader (*An enthusiastic and vocal supporter of someone or something*)

I can truthfully say that a big part of my current success in Dominica is down to all the wonderful people I have mentioned thus far but the star must go to my sister Liza Collaire. From day one she has not only supported my endeavours but has also allowed me access to her many contacts in Dominica. Liza promoted me to all her business contacts and has been there at each one of my book launches and events. At my most recent event, held at the Prevo Cinemall in Roseau, where I did a joint event with the Dominica Association of Industry and Commerce (DAIC), my sister helped me to set up the room and greeted guests as they arrived. Liza had such an impact that she received special thanks from Brenton Hilaire, the President of the DAIC, who specifically praised her for the warm welcome she extended to everyone.

Dominica Association of Industry and Commerce (DAIC)

One of the key things I believe is the importance of aligning yourself with an organisation that shares some of the values and vision that you also hold. DAIC is the leading private sector representative body in Dominica with membership across various sectors and industries. It is responsible for the representation of private sector interests in the country. Joining the Chamber was one of the best things I have done when it comes to my professional life. When I attended the first networking event with the DAIC, I instinctively knew I was in the right place. Chatting to other business contacts, exchanging business cards or LinkedIn contact details made me feel right at home! The Executive Director at the time, Lizra Fabien, a lovely, talented young lady, was very encouraging. Immediately I was involved in a variety of events and I started to build my contacts. I was also invited to be part of a panel for an International Women's Day event and to be part of discussions and interviews for a variety of projects.

Board Membership

At the DAIC Annual General Meeting (AGM) in 2021 they were looking for new Board Members. This was not a face-to-face meeting, with Covid restrictions still in place it was conducted via Zoom. The Chair requested any suggestions for Board Membership and when Tamara Lowe-James, Island Manager for Tropical Shipping (Antigua and Barbuda) put my name forward I was so surprised! We had only met briefly previously but I was happy to receive her vote. Then they asked for someone to second that suggestion and it all went very quiet. I remember thinking "Well no one really knows me, sit tight and see what happens" when suddenly a voice said "I second that!" I believe it was Evadney Esprit, who is the General Manager of Do It Center (Dominica). I felt jubilant to be a Board Member and Director of the Chamber. It felt fabulous to achieve one of my goals.

Being a Member of the DAIC has definitely contributed to my successful integration into the business community in Dominica. At the AGM in 2022, held at the Fort Young Hotel in Roseau, the Prime Minister of Dominica attended, together with members of his cabinet, and I was able to meet him personally for the first time. My membership has also helped me to visit and create relationships with local businesses, take part in key discussions regarding issues that face the private sector, work in partnership with key stakeholders of behalf of the DAIC, and have a joint launch event with the Chamber to build my brand and increase my visibility within the business community.

Rotary Club of Dominica

When I joined the DAIC I knew that I was joining a business community that I wanted to be part of. However, I joined the Rotary Club of Dominica (RCD) for completely different reasons as I had heard that it was more about volunteering to solve problems in the community. Rotary International has a global network of 1.4 million neighbours, friends and leaders who volunteer their skills and resources to solve problems and address community needs. The RCD was officially chartered on 1 July 1974 with twenty-three members and it currently has over forty members. It is a community-based organisation made up of volunteers. Through being a member of the Rotary I have given back to my community by volunteering but have also attended events that have enabled members to network and get to know each other better. To date I have made a presentation about a career in HR to children at the Dominica Grammar School, served lunch at the Grotto Home for the Homeless, and volunteered at Portsmouth Hospital during the Volunteer Optometric Services to Humanity (VOSH) Eye Mission. I have also attended many social events, including a Christmas party, which have been great fun. I attend Rotary Fellowship gatherings which provide an opportunity for Rotarians to meet, sometimes at another Rotarian's house, or at a local venue. It's a chance to get to know each other, build friendships and socialise.

I have attended two Investiture Ceremonies in Rotary, which involved electing a new President and Board of Directors, as well as fundraising for the Club service projects, an awards presentation, and most recently a VOSH celebration lunch at Cabrits National Park.

Spending time with my fellow Rotarians and socialising has made my life richer, more fun, and interesting. Once again, as a returnee to Dominica, if I had not joined DAIC and RCD I would not have had the opportunity to meet our politicians and captains of industry.

CHAPTER 16
Reflecting and taking stock

It was time to reflect on what I had achieved and where I was in my life. I had put a lot of energy, finance, and effort into creating what I wanted in Dominica but as the U2 song says *"I have climbed the highest mountains, I have run through the fields, but I still haven't found, what I am looking for."* I still hadn't gained any paid employment in Dominica, although I was working sporadically with clients elsewhere in the world. Unfortunately, the combination of Covid and relocating had a bad impact on my business. Much of my self-esteem and feeling of accomplishment comes from my work, it has always made me feel good about myself, given me a sense of worth and purpose, but now my skills were not being fully utilised and it began to get me down.

It was fast approaching September 2021 and my sixtieth birthday. My birthday plans before moving to the Caribbean consisted of a trip to Hawaii, somewhere I have always wanted to visit, and then a huge party - after all you are only sixty once! We were just coming out of the Covid pandemic and there were still some restrictions in place, so Hawaii wasn't to be, but the thought of not having my children, grandchildren and friends around me to celebrate made me feel very sad. I spoke to my husband and children about how I was feeling and my children urged me to come to the UK.

And so it was decided that I would spend my sixtieth birthday in the UK. I missed my children and grandchildren so much but our regular chats via Facetime and WhatsApp really helped, as they kept that precious link with my family; we could see the beloved faces of our beautiful grandchildren and hear their joyous laughter, but I longed to give them a big hug. Also, in the UK we had built friendships that spanned decades so sometimes the front doorbell would ring and a friend or neighbour would just call around for a coffee or a visit. This didn't happen in Dominica; we didn't really know our neighbours very well and had not established the kind of familiarity with friends who felt that they could just pop round as they were passing. My husband couldn't accompany me because we still had work to complete on the house, so he paid for my ticket. My children looked forward to my visit and we had long chats about what we were going to do when I arrived. I was so excited, I sang every day and skipped around the house *"shaking what my momma gave me"* as the song says!

Being recognised by my profession

In August 2021, just after I had made the decision to visit the UK and booked my ticket, I received some wonderful and unexpected news. Firstly, I received an email to say that I had been nominated for Chartered Companion status of the Chartered Institute of Personnel and Development (CIPD). I must admit that I was overcome by this news. I joined the Institute in 1996 as a student and never dreamed that I would achieve the level of Chartered Companion, it is something that I am extremely proud of. I was invited to attend the People Management Awards Ceremony on Tuesday 28 September to be held at the Grosvenor House Hotel, Park Lane, London. It was a tremendous evening, full of glitz and glamour.

Chartered Companion is one of the highest levels of recognition in the world of HR and people development. The CIPD's select group of Chartered Companions are exceptional leaders who have a proven track record within organisations and have demonstrated exceptional impact on the profession over their careers. This is the highest accolade and level of membership awarded by the CIPD professional body and the selection of individuals to enter this group is made directly by the CIPD Board.

On the night of the event I arrived in my sparkling silver dress, champagne in hand, feeling so proud to be there amongst my peers. There were over six hundred people in this beautiful room. I reflected on how I had changed my career from the recruitment field and returned to university in the evening as a working parent, two evenings a week after work, then finding time to study at weekends between housework and shopping and taking care of my family's needs. I'd gone on to join the CIPD Committee and subsequently became the Branch Chair. This involved organising celebrations at a local level for the CIPD centenary, working for the CIPD as a consultant, and facilitating events remotely and in person to international audiences. I was made very welcome whenever I visited the head office in Wimbledon and received tremendous support over the years from my CIPD colleagues. On the night so many people came to my table to wish me well, including the CIPD CEO, Peter Cheese, who has always been supportive of me throughout my HR career. To arrive at this moment, seeing my name up on the screen, confirmation of my Chartered Companion membership - to receive this honour and recognition for my work was a life affirming experience and the pinnacle of my HR career.

I was also contacted by Coral Horn, founder of The Enterprise Visions Awards (EVA), one of the premier ladies' business awards, to say that I had been nominated for the Training and Coaching Awards, but you needed votes as well as the other criteria. I was over the moon to be nominated and proceeded to contact each client that I had ever worked with and all my contacts on LinkedIn, asking them to vote for me. It was a tough contest with over six hundred entries. At each stage of the process you needed people to vote for you and I made sure that I used my social media platforms to keep my nomination fresh in everyone's mind. I eventually received the news that I had been shortlisted and the next phase was a panel interview which was completed via Zoom, as we still had to consider the implications of Covid.

When I received the news that I was shortlisted for the award I was so happy - happy and optimistic! Whether I won or not, I was going to be there on the night, drinking in the atmosphere amongst other business professionals. On the night of 24 September 2021, I was at the award ceremony held at the iconic Empress Ballroom of the Winter Gardens in Blackpool. The atmosphere was amazing, you could feel that everyone there on the night was wishing everyone well, there was no rivalry, just support and love. At my table we had all introduced ourselves and knew what category each person was shortlisted for. Each time a category was called for someone on our table, we would look at them, cross our fingers, then commiserate if they didn't win or cheer at the top of our lungs if they did! My category was called and I sat there, my heart beating fast. The list of other nominees was hard to beat, every single person deserved that award. My fellow guests at our table all looked at me expectantly and I held my breath. When my name was called there was a loud cheer and up I went onto the stage, in my red organza ball gown, feeling like the Queen of Sheba! I made a short speech, thanking everyone and sharing my journey of how I arrived at this moment in my life. The response was wonderful, lots of laughter, acknowledgement, appreciation, and support. It was a fabulous evening. When I returned to my hotel room that night I lay on the bed in my red ball gown, clutching my award with a big smile on my face!

This was only the beginning of the most wonderful birthday that I could wish for. I had arrived in the UK a week before my birthday and my son met me at the airport with flowers, followed by lunch at Carluccio's. Afterwards I was whisked off to the Midland Hotel where my daughter had organised a suite for me to stay in. I was then ushered to the Midland Spa for a day of pampering, joined by my sister-in-law and partner in crime, Pat Strachan. And it didn't end there. My children had booked a sumptuous meal for me at Mr Cooper's, where they joined me along with their partners, my sister-in-law, and grandchildren. At the end of the night, I was presented with a beautiful gift of a specially engraved gold and silver bracelet, which I treasure. I was so moved by the effort they had put into making my sixtieth special that tears came to my eyes. It was a perfect, more than I could have hoped for. My children did me proud and really made me feel loved and special. A mother could not hope for more perfect and loving children. Breakfast the following morning with the grandchildren was a hilarious affair. I also spent some time with each of my children at their homes, being spoilt rotten. Before leaving the hotel I had another surprise. My lovely friend Candace

Edwards, who lives in Spain, had organised a gift to be delivered to me at the hotel.

My friends also made my sixtieth special. After leaving the Midland Hotel, I stayed with my friend Edith, which was my base, and then my friend Julie De Luca invited me to spend a few days at her home in Bury, and my sister-in-law Pat Strachan invited me to spend some time with her in Preston. I met with the "Famous Five" at a restaurant in Bury, where my five fabulous friends from university had organised a lunch. I met with friends Marlene and Norma for dinner in Urmston, and my sister-in-law and her friend arranged a weekend away for me, complete with celebratory wine and a night at the theatre. We laughed and danced all night. I also met friends individually, such as Jane Hanson and Jo Harding, for meals and catch ups, and friends who couldn't be there sent gifts and cards. I had a fabulous time, and it was just a whirlwind of fun, fun, fun!

During my visit something suddenly hit me like a bolt from the blue - I no longer had a house in the UK! When I thought about my life there, it was the halcyon memories of days gone by, family get togethers, sitting in the garden with friends. The reality is that I could spend time with my children at their homes, visit my friends at their homes, but I didn't have anywhere that I could lock the door, kick my shoes off and put the TV on that was mine. My home was now in the Caribbean.

I spoke at length to my children, their partners, and my friends about my transition to Dominica and how I was finding it difficult to adjust and settle. When I arrived back in Urmston, where I had lived for such a long time, there was a feeling of familiarity and coming home, just walking around the streets. I went to have lunch at my favourite restaurant, Lilly's, and they remembered me and asked how my move to the Caribbean was going. In the NatWest bank, where I had banked for over thirty years, I walked in and received smiles of welcome and lots of questions about my new home. It was wonderful to feel so welcomed.

During my last few days in the UK before returning to Dominica, I spent some time with my son in law, Anthony Boyode, who works in Corporate & International Trade Sales for Lloyds Banking group. Anthony really believes in me and my abilities. We spoke for a while about how I could make living in Dominica work for me. He made some excellent suggestions about how I could market myself better, looking at different avenues for my skill set and comparing me with some well-known influencers, who he felt that I could learn from in order to develop myself in different ways. He really made me feel motivated, which helped me to create the right mindset to return to Dominica and create the life that I wanted there.

Unfortunately, towards the end of my visit my mother-in-law died. My husband immediately flew from Dominica to join me in the UK for her funeral in Preston, where children, grandchildren and great grandchildren gathered. It felt like the end of an era. My father had passed away ten years previously, Errol's father had died seven years ago, and now his mother had also gone. He was devastated. Indeed, it was a sad time for us all and many visitors came to pay their respects and mourn her passing at the family home in Preston, where we stayed for the final week of my visit.

Change of mindset

The visit to the UK was just what I needed. I thoroughly enjoyed every moment but it clarified the fact that when I visited the UK I no longer had a home there. My home was in Dominica and my husband was very happy there, so the chance of us going back to the UK together was remote. I took stock of what I had and what I felt was missing so that I could fill the gaps.

We live in a beautiful part of Dominica; the area is sought after and the houses are lovely. The house was designed to my husband's specification, although he did consult me along the way! But, like most relationships, you know what your partner's skills and abilities are and I knew that Errol's design would be amazing. And sure enough, it is! The house is set in a quarter of an acre of land. Strangers pass by and get their cameras out to take photographs, telling us that if we ever want to sell the house they would be at the front of the queue. Inside the house Errol had ensured that I was comfortable, with integrated mosquito screens on every window, so I was now safe from flying, biting things! My mum and my sister lived about an hour away and I visited regularly. The big question was, what was missing from my life? I am a social butterfly, always having somewhere to go and plenty of friends to call upon. I missed my children and the innocent laughter of my grandchildren, their exuberance and unconditional love, and my friends who have known me for decades and love me warts and all!

However, my plan for building my professional brand in the Caribbean could not bear fruit immediately because on 18 November 2021 my beloved mother died. I realised that there had been a purpose for me to return to Dominica because I spent that final year with her before she died, precious time that could not be measured in gold. Liza had returned to Dominica ten years before me, my father had passed away, and we were worried about Mum being in her seventies and needing more support. One of my younger sisters, Sharon, lived with her but to my mum it was Liza and I, the eldest, that she would listen to, whereas my younger sisters were her babies and still needed guidance from her. So, Liza came to Dominica and took over the reins that my father had held, organising the household, including mum's finances etc., and I was in regular contact via telephone, contributed financially and visited when I could. Errol and I, together with Liza, and Sharon and her daughters, made sure that mum was comfortable and well cared for.

Upon my arrival in Dominica in October 2020 Mum was so glad to have me there, she now had three of her four daughters with her and she loved it. However, I didn't realise that Mum's health was failing. She was suffering from Type 2 Diabetes and was getting forgetful, somewhat natural at eighty-five years old, I thought. I would visit every other week and chat to her on the phone in between times. One day Liza took me to one side and explained that Mum's health was not that great and it would be good for me to spend time more time with her whilst I still had the opportunity. In my mind I thought we had years to go and that when I had established myself, I would then spend more time with Mum. However, Liza's warning was timely, as the more time I spent with Mum I realised that her memory really was failing; she was aware of it and would ask me if I thought she was getting too forgetful. I asked her if she was happy and she said yes, she was very happy, living with her family who loved her. I then said, "Well Mum, if you are happy then nothing else matters."

I am so grateful to my sister for giving me that warning, I started to focus on my mum more and building a business took a back seat. I would pick Mum up, or my sisters would bring her to Roseau and I would meet them there. We would go out together for day trips, have lunch together etc. It was lovely, with Mum telling me stories about her childhood and her experiences of life. Little did I know how short-lived these trips would be. The week before she died I took Mum to Scott's Head, a lovely little village, and then for lunch at the eco-resort of Jungle Bay Dominica, and afterwards we went swimming at Portsmouth, Dominica's second biggest town. She spent Sunday reading her bible in the garden before having a late breakfast and we then drove her to see her brother in Castle Bruce before taking her home to La Plaine. She kept thanking us for a brilliant weekend, saying how much she had enjoyed herself.

On Thursday 18 November 2021 my sister Liza rang me in tears to say that our mother had died. My husband just put me in the car and drove me to La Plaine. I cried all the way there, because physically my mum seemed fine and I couldn't believe that we had been laughing and joking just a few days ago and now she had gone. My Mum died with both my sisters Liza and Sharon looking after her, and my niece Malika helping as well. She had said she wasn't feeling well and they were all trying to make her feel better. In the end she collapsed in Liza's arms as she was rubbing her back. When I arrived, she was lying on the settee looking so peaceful, as though she had just fallen asleep. She was still warm and I was able to give her a hug and lie next to her for the last time.

My Mum was the most constant person in my life, apart from my husband. I didn't meet my father for the first time until I was six years old, however, Mum was always there with her unstinting and unconditional love. She was the best of mothers, making sure each of her four girls were loved and cherished. My mum left her mark on everyone she met. We had so many visitors after the news of her death spread amongst the community in La Plaine that the front garden of our family home was full of people standing there talking about her and paying their respects. Months after she had gone people would just turn up, asking for her, not believing she was no longer there. The local priest and some of the congregation came to the house the day of her death, and prayers were said and her favourite hymn sung. She insisted that her burial place would be Castle Bruce, where she was born and where the St. Rose family are buried. My sisters asked me to do the eulogy for Mum, just like I had done for my father ten years before, and I tried to capture the amazing woman, wife, mother, grandmother, and great grandmother that was my mum. My children, together with my sister Susan and her son, came to Dominica to help send Mum off in style.

Recently, Mum's local church had a celebration Mass for her. It was so wonderful to hear the congregation singing her praises. She was a Church Elder, providing counselling, mentoring and advice to the younger members. Young married men praised Mum for the advice she had given them. Young women praised her for the life skills she had shared. Mum is sorely missed by all. Everyone said that they used to love snuggling up to her because my mum loved to smell nice. First there was the shower, then the powder, and finally the perfume; she always smelled so sweet and fresh. Gone but never forgotten. The roots of who I am come from my parents. Mum's kindness, generosity, integrity, sense of fun, capacity to make everyone feel loved and special, and her resilience through life's hardships, are an example to all.

Something happened not long after my mum's death which reassured me that her loving and reassuring presence would always be with me. I live an hour away from the family home in La Plaine and getting there and back in the dark can prove challenging due to a lack of road signs, dirt tracks rather than roads, and no lights in some areas. Dominica is lush and green and the roads are very twisty, with sheer drops. You can't take your eyes from the road for a minute or you could end up in a ravine, or over a cliff. I had been driving back and forth most days leading up to the funeral as there was a lot to organise. I would drive home at night on pitch black roads, in parts alongside steep precipices, or ditches down to a river. I had driven this route quite a few times and although it was dark and wet, I felt confident that I would get home to Roseau safely. But I was anxious about the funeral, and obviously grieving for my mum, and unbeknownst to me I took a wrong turning.

Normally the main road widens as it gets nearer to Roseau but as I kept driving the road became more and more narrow, so much so that at one point there was vegetation touching both sides of the car and long tree branches scraping along the roof. I put on the full beam and I could see that I was encased in bushes and trees. Ahead of me were big potholes, and puddles of water so huge that in parts I could hardly see the road. It felt like the front of the car was submerged in water. My heart was beating very fast and I started to panic, because in Dominica often you are driving and without warning you will just see a sheer drop at the side of you, or you turn your car around in a small space only to see a river in front of you. It is important to always keep your eye on the road. My main fear was of turning left or right and ending up down a precipice. There were no road signs, no lights, just pitch black, lots of vegetation and water everywhere. At one point I was sure I saw a snake and some manicou, Dominican opossums. Thankfully, I had a full tank of petrol and my one thought was to just keep going.

My journey home should have taken about an hour and my sisters had rung Errol to see if I had arrived safely. When he told them I had not, they began to panic. I had left them at 9pm and it was now 10.30pm! My sister rang my mobile phone to see if I was okay and I just said, "Can't talk now, have to get out of this pool of water." My husband also rang and I confessed that I didn't have the faintest idea of where I was. I just kept following the road. I was very scared, I must admit, and at one point I felt myself going into full panic mode, but then I thought of Mum and I knew she would not let anything bad happen to me. I felt her warmth, as though she was there with me, and I felt much calmer. Eventually, I came across some houses, and a man and woman were standing outside in nightgowns, chatting. I had ended up in an area called Layou where, on the radio just a few days ago, they had reported that parts of the Layou River were impassable and blocked due to heavy rainfall. I wound my window down and asked, "Excuse me, can you tell me the way to Roseau?" The woman peered into the car and seeing me sitting there alone, she asked "Papa Bondye, is it only you alone in the car at this time of night?" "Yes," I said, feeling on the verge of tears.

I was given directions to the Layou Bridge, which involved going across a quarry and finally ending up on the Edward Le Blanc highway. I can't tell you how relieved I was to get back to familiarity! I arrived home at midnight and it took me quite a while to calm down, but to this day I know that my mum was with me that night.

CHAPTER 17
Rediscovering my Prime

My mother's death had an impact on us all but one thought uppermost in my mind was the fact that she lived life to the full and she spread joy and laughter wherever she went. I had a discussion with my sisters after her funeral and we all agreed that Mum had an inkling that she was going. She kept repeating the fact that she did not want to be buried in La Plaine, where she currently lived, but must be buried next to her family, the St. Roses, in Castle Bruce where she was born. Although we miss her and wish could spend just one more day with her, we think she was ready and prepared for the final journey.

Mum was extremely proud of my achievements and always encouraged me to push forward and to utilise all my talent and skills, and after her death I decided to take stock of where I was in my life and, more pertinently, where I wanted to be. A big part of what I do is coach and mentor others, helping them to achieve success. I decided to do some self-coaching and look at my vision for the future - where exactly did I want to go in Dominica, and what did I want to achieve?

When coaching others I use the Wheel of Life, which rates different aspects of your life, for example physical environment, health, fun and recreation, romance, personal growth, career, etc. I completed some self-assessment and decided to focus on health, fun and recreation, and personal growth.

Health and wellbeing

I am a woman in her early sixties and have struggled with my weight most of my life, going from a UK size 10 in my teens to a size 16 in my more mature years. The women in my family tend to be curvaceous. Hypertension runs in the family too, with both parents suffering from this chronic disease. In an article by The Caribbean Public Health Agency (CARPHA), published on 17 May 2021, their Executive Director Dr. Joy St John says "The Caribbean region has the highest prevalence of raised blood pressure in the Americas ranging from a high of 27.1% to a low of 20.9%." She adds "It is a cause for concern and action when in all

Caribbean countries, hypertension is above the regional average for the Americas."

By the time I moved to Dominica I had lived with hypertension for a number of years. My husband, who has remained approximately the same weight and clothes size since we met in 1980, did not have that issue. However, we had gone from eating a diet of steamed sea bass, prawns, grilled chops, and steamed vegetables to a much richer diet in the Caribbean. In Manchester I attended the David Lloyd gym at least three times a week, now I was taking the occasional walk or hike with my husband. The takeaway food in Dominica is of large proportions, to the extent that when we first arrived we would buy one meal and share it because typically, for a lunch of approximately 30 XCD (East Caribbean Dollars), less than £10, it consisted of rice, yams, figs, steamed vegetables or salad, macaroni cheese, peas, and a meat or fish of your choice. This meal is about 2000 calories, nearly a full day's calories for a healthy female. We did try to resist falling into the trap of having this for our lunch and kept sharing it, however, my husband had designed our garden so that we had an abundance of all the fruit trees he had loved when growing up in Jamaica: pineapples, mangoes, soursop, guava, sugar cane, melons, jackfruit, ackee, and so on. Within a short space of time our trees were bearing fruit and I was making my own juice. Our neighbours were very kind, sharing their sorrel fruit crop with us, which also makes a lovely juice. What I didn't realise was that the Caribbean fruits are high in sugar and the delicious juices that we both enjoyed so much were taking us over our daily sugar limit, in addition to a diet high in starch from vegetables such as yams, dasheen, plantain, etc. Before long we went for our check up with the local doctor and were both diagnosed as being pre-diabetic, which meant we had to make drastic changes to our diet. For example, one ripe mango can contain up to forty-six grams of sugar, and we had unknowingly been juicing them daily thinking they were good for us. Lifestyle changes were required and no more juicing, better to eat the whole fruit as it is.

I remember sitting with my doctor as he listed all the things I couldn't have anymore. No soda, no wine, no fruit drinks, no alcohol, no bread, no chocolate, no sweets of any kind, no wheat, no rice, no pasta, no biscuits. I looked at him in appalled silence and asked was there anything left that I could eat or drink? He said you can drink water and eat fish, chicken and turkey with green leafy vegetables and have nuts for a snack. This was his advice for reversing Type 2 Diabetes. Well after my consultation I arrived home with a very long face. The days of sitting on our veranda in the evening, enjoying a sumptuous meal and a glass of red wine with hubby, seemed like a thing of the past. It has taken a period of adjustment and I have made some changes, albeit not quite as drastic as those outlined by my doctor. We do still have wine and chocolate, but as a treat rather than every day.

Another key learning point for me and my husband was that because we had spent the majority of our life in the UK, and specifically Manchester, which is known for its grey and rainy weather, our vitamin D count was extremely low. Also, there is growing evidence that vitamin D has a role in sleep regulation and I have suffered from insomnia for most of my adult life. My doctor in Dominica has given me medication for the deficiency and advised lying in the sun for short periods of time, especially with my stomach area exposed, to reap the full benefit. I can honestly say that I now sleep for eight hours and awake rested for the first time in my life. My sleep pattern has changed so much that my husband comes to check that I am still alive, he is not used to an Olive who sleeps!

In addition to healthy eating, we go hiking. Dominica is known for opportunities to hike. We recently went to the Boeri Lake, the highest lake in Dominica at an altitude of 2,850 ft. (869 m) and because of its height it is often shrouded in mist. We climbed the trail, which is a little over a mile, and takes approximately forty-five minutes there and another forty-five minutes back. It is breathtakingly beautiful and definitely worth a trip. Another hike that I would recommend is going to the Freshwater Lake, the largest of Dominica's four lakes, located at just over 2,500 ft (762 m) above sea level. It is an amazing experience as it is very cool up there. When you leave Roseau, you are wearing shorts or a summer dress and by the time you arrive at Freshwater Lake a cardigan or jacket is required. We have visited a few times now and it never disappoints, with its beautiful green landscape and mist shrouded lake. We now try to go for a good walk at least a few times a week, or just go the beach for a swim. Living in Dominica encourages an outdoor lifestyle.

Wellbeing – happy in your own skin

Life in Dominica can be satisfying and enjoyable once you come to the realisation that you need patience and the understanding that all things take time. Don't try to change Dominica, accept and create your own space. When expats compare Dominica to the UK the Dominicans say, "But this is not the UK, you are now in Dominica." I have to pay for healthcare here as there is no NHS type service, but because the population is mainly Black all the ailments that are particular to my race have been focused on, and there is a better understanding of my needs as a Black person that is not there in the UK. For example, the information regarding vitamin D and its impact, as well as knowledge of Caribbean foods and herbs and their medicinal impact. The doctors here understand the Black person's physiology better and are therefore able to pinpoint issues that are not focused on in the UK where we are part of a minority. Basic things like giving blood in the UK involved a lot of painful, prodding and poking, because there was always a struggle to find a vein in my dark skin. Here in Dominica there has never been a problem, perhaps because they are used to the darker skin pigmentation. I feel healthier, sleep better, and have a sense of well-being that I did not have in the UK. Don't get me wrong, when it comes to major surgery and advanced medical treatment it has to be the UK, but for treatment specifically for Black people and understanding the specific needs of the Black population, there is greater understanding in the Caribbean.

Black is beautiful

As a Black woman I can truthfully say that I never felt beautiful in the UK, and speaking to other Black women, it was obvious that I was not the only one who felt that way. Everything is geared towards blonde beauty and blue eyes. I remember commenting at an event once, about how beautiful Michelle Obama was, and there was total silence. In the UK, Black skin does not equate to beauty. As a child at school, we were always put at the back when it came to photographs. During the Covid epidemic they filmed nurses working hard every day but in a nation where thirty percent of the nurses and midwives are Black, the film crew managed to film every day and somehow not show one Black nurse or sister on the ward. My sister-in-law who worked in the medical field commented on it, as did every Black person I asked about this. But this is typical of how things are with selective filming. This is how things were when I was growing up in Blackburn in the 1970's and 80's. I optimistically thought that things would be better for my children and grandchildren but unfortunately it remains the same.

Serlina Boyd created *Cocoa Girl* magazine to instil confidence in Black girls. She says "Imagine, as a child, not being able to find anyone who looks like you in the glossy magazines. No role models." This is exactly how six-year-old Faith felt and her mum, Serlina, decided it was time to change the narrative. Together with Faith she designed and published the UK's first Black girls' magazine, *Cocoa Girl*, and *Cocoa Boy* soon followed. Black children now have a magazine that represents them and helps them feel good about themselves. My son Ricky was also searching for some representations about Black history and asked, "Where are our Kings and Queens, our scientists and philosophers?" These are very rarely mentioned, it's as though our entire history has not been acknowledged. My son spent five years researching Black history and wrote a children's book called *African Kings*. Once it was published, nine schools contacted him to come and present his findings to school children. On arriving at his first school, a little Black girl looked at him and asked him if he was the speaker for the evening. When he said yes, she said "Oh that's great! Someone who looks like me!"

There is a real thirst amongst Black children in the UK for some positive representation of themselves in the newspapers, TV, and the media in general. I spent many years in the UK, both personally and professionally, and had a good life there, so I am not knocking the UK, I am just pointing out some issues that need to be addressed so that everyone can take their rightful place in society.

On the contrary, I do feel beautiful living in the Caribbean! Firstly, it is wonderful to walk around and not feel like a minority and that you stand out just because of the colour of your skin. I remember having to get myself mentally ready when going to events in the UK, as usually I was either the only Black person, or there would be just one or two of us. I would prepare myself to fit in and be as amenable as possible, dealing with the micro aggressions of everyday life. That is not an issue in the Caribbean. I walk in with a confidence and comfort that I did not have in the UK. As I write this book, I am in my sixty-second year and for the first time in my life I feel beautiful, not just for a moment like I felt on my wedding day, or in small snapshot moments, but every day. Every day I go out in Dominica I receive compliments on my beautiful black skin, my smile, my dimples, my physique. It's not just me, every woman I speak to feels this sense of appreciation for just being who she is. It is a wonderful, empowering feeling, which makes you stand that bit taller, walk with a swing in your step and smile from the inside. This feeling of being happy with who I am as a woman reminds me of the poem by Maya Angelou, *Rise*. "*Does my sexiness upset you? Does it come as a surprise, that I dance like I've got diamonds at the meeting of my thighs?*" This beautiful, amazing poem resonates with me on so many levels.

Fun and recreation

When it comes to activity, Dominica can pack a powerful punch! Coming out of Covid restrictions there is so much happening. In 2022 we attended the Dominica Jazz 'N Creole Festival at Fort Shirley in the Cabrits National Park. Dominica's annual World Creole Festival held in Roseau every October is fabulous and I was lucky enough to be invited to join in the celebrations by one of my clients who had a corporate box. And of course, every February we celebrate Carnival!

On a personal note, it is impossible to replace our long-term friends in the UK, however, we have made some lovely friends here, with pool parties, balls to attend, weekends at our friends' country home, and our neighbour inviting us to his family celebrations. Life is looking up.

Also, we are both now in our sixties and sometimes just sitting down and enjoying our beautiful home and garden is all we need. We have an abundance of tropical flowers, hummingbirds dart around the garden, the area we live in is peaceful and beautiful, and sometimes I have to pinch myself as I survey my lovely surroundings. I feel that my cup runneth over. My friend Marieke coined a phrase which I feel says it all. When her friends look at the pictures of Dominica and exclaim at its beauty, she says, "I live where you holiday"!

Personal growth/development

"Personal development or self-improvement consists of activities that develop a person's capabilities and potential, build human capital, facilitate employability and enhance quality of life and the realisation of dreams and aspirations."

This description is taken from Wikipedia and encompasses all I want to achieve in Dominica. After earning my master's degree in 2011 I had no further desire to pursue more academic qualifications, but I will always keep on learning via other means - books, webinars, events, podcasts, videos, etc. - there is no excuse in this day and age! One of the important things I advocate is to surround yourself with the right people. Part of my personal growth in Dominica included joining the right networks, getting involved and making a contribution.

Integration

When I sit and reflect on the past two years, I realise that I have worked through the Kubler Ross Change Curve. Originally developed to explain the grieving process, it can also be used to help people understand their reactions to great change or upheaval.

It begins with the feeling of shock, when the change first happens, then denial, anger, bargaining, depression, and eventually acceptance, where you start to experiment, explore new ideas and integrate. I feel that this is where I am at the moment. I walk around Roseau and it is very rare that I don't meet an acquaintance, just to exchange pleasantries. If I fancy going out to lunch, I now have a few friends I can invite to join me. Being a Director of both DAIC and the Rotary Club means that I have a full diary with business meetings and community led events. There is rarely have a week when I am not involved in some sort of activity.

CHAPTER 18
Success is never achieved alone

The most successful people always have a team of supporters who have assisted them to achieve their goals. Apart from my family and particularly my husband, who has always been by my side, providing support and financial assistance when necessary, and my children and my sister Liza, I have had help, support, guidance, and advice from people who I had never met before moving to the Caribbean.

Alex Haley, the author of the book *Roots,* had a picture in his office of a turtle sitting on top of a fence. He kept it there as a reminder that if you see a turtle on a fence post, you know he had some help. This helped him not to forget the people who had some influence in his success.

I have achieved a modicum of success in my new life in Dominica, but I wouldn't be where I am today without the support and wise counsel of a few special people. Each person that demonstrated some interest in my journey took time to open doors for me and assisted in creating opportunities. They have had an important part in bringing me to the current day and my integration into Dominica's professional environment, leading me to my ultimate goal of paid employment. Taking some time to reflect, I have identified five specific types of people who, by bringing their abilities, connections, and skills to bear, have influenced my successful integration. Their interventions have been part of the essential ingredients in my rediscovering my prime.

Firstly, a *connector* is someone who enables contact between you and someone else. This is not just passing on a phone number, as in "ring so and so". This person makes the connection and follows up. "How did that meeting go? Was it successful? What else can I do to help to build this relationship between you and this person?" I found that initially I was given a lot of phone numbers by well-meaning people but a call out of the blue from a complete stranger is not always conducive to creating a connection. Someone taking their time to assist is more beneficial, especially if they understand what you are looking for and what you need and can match you with the right person.

One of my main connectors is Sam Raphael, the owner of Jungle Bay Resort and Spa. As a successful entrepreneur, Sam is renowned for his business acumen and his generosity as a coach and mentor to other businesses. He has been instrumental in making me some valuable connections. On a recent visit I asked whether he would stock my book, *The Power of You*, in his bookshop at the resort and he agreed without hesitation. Every time I visit Jungle Bay, Sam makes the effort to help me to make and build my connections.

Secondly, a *facilitator* is a person who makes an action or a process easier. When I became a member of the DAIC it was for the sole purpose of making contacts in the business world and establishing myself as a businesswoman. In Dominica they are fiercely loyal to each other and promote everything Dominican. If a choice had to be made between a local consultant and me, they would always choose the person they know. It takes time to build trust and a reputation. I was finding the process of building my brand challenging but on meeting Lizra Fabien, in her role as Executive Director of the Chamber, I met a kindred spirit. Lizra took me under her wing, making sure that I was aware of all the benefits of being a Chamber member and taking advantage of all the opportunities available to me. I was not the only person that Lizra assisted in this way, all members who required help were given it. I spoke to Lizra regarding my goal to establish my business and the challenges I was facing. Connecting with Lizra has been extremely beneficial to me both personally and professionally. She has made the process of integrating into Dominica's private sector businesses a reality and not just a dream. She helped me to be more visible by inviting me be part of a panel of professional businesswomen in Dominica on International Women's Day, to present a session on Leadership to entrepreneurs, and by encouraging me to attend the right events hosted by DAIC and other bodies.

Lizra has her own consultancy called *Progressism* and I have been a guest speaker at her excellent events. She has recently taken on a new role as the Caribbean Projects Manager for the Organization of American States (OAS), dealing with "Economically Empowered Women for Equitable and Resilient Societies". We remain in contact and are planning some future projects together.

Thirdly, an *initiator* is someone who causes a process or action to begin. I was very fortunate to have three people who initiated actions which led directly to business opportunities. One initiator identified an organisation in their network which could use my skills and abilities and wrote to them on my behalf. Another initiator had won a contract and brought me in to work with them as an associate; this contract was working in partnership on a HR Gap Analysis for the Dominican Government. Another person who falls under this category worked as an extremely successful consultant herself and gave me the opportunity to work with her as an associate. Later, when she gained a permanent role, she gave me the opportunity to work with her at her new organisation.

My key initiators are: from day one of arriving in Dominica, Tina Alexander MBE, Executive Director at Lifeline Ministries Inc., has worked to support and help me, initiating links that have been extremely beneficial; Cecily Lees, retired Solicitor and entrepreneur, who initiated my first professional business meeting with a large, well-known company which resulted in me delivering some leadership development workshops; Natasha Yeeloy Labad, Chief Executive Officer at Outsource Development Studio Inc., gave me the opportunity to work with her, introducing me to her HR contacts and working in partnership on a joint project. By their actions these three women started me on my road map to business success in Dominica.

The fourth type of person is a *cheerleader*, someone who encourages and openly supports the success of a person or cause. In Dominica, my main cheerleaders are my husband and my sister Liza. This includes accompanying me to my early presentations, my husband driving me there and my sister giving me support, but also encouraging people to read my book and making sure that everyone they meet is aware of me and what I can provide on a professional basis. Steve Vidal, from Kairi FM, took time to introduce me to his contacts, two of whom invited me onto their radio programmes, giving me the opportunity to reach a different audience. These are Vanessa Bruno, host of *Hot Topics*, and Olivia Odileke, host of *Live Your Life*. I was also fortunate to be invited by Cuthbert Joseph to promote my first book on his radio programme, *CB's Corner*, on the New England Television Network.

Later on, the managers and leaders of the various organisations that I have worked with have also become my cheerleaders, promoting my services to their contacts.

And finally, we have the *navigators*, those people who have assisted me in finding direction in my new life in Dominica when I first arrived. Initially I was very much immersed in UK culture whilst expecting to fit into Dominican society quickly and make my mark. I needed advice on the best method of integrating myself and understanding why just being "Olive" wasn't going to cut it. I had to be a different Olive, with a shift in my behaviour, more patience and understanding, but also to take a step back and observe, and learn to pick up on subtle nuances. In other words, learn and adapt. I was very fortunate to have many women who were prepared to give me guidance and good advice, then and to the current day. There are many people in Dominica who have taken the time to steer my ship in the right direction, helping me to navigate the sometimes-turbulent waters of Dominica and my new life.

Digital Nomad

Covid has forced us all to revaluate our life choices and how and where we work. The impacts of Covid are far reaching and we are still feeling the effects now, in 2023.

From my point of view, Covid has made me a Digital Nomad, which means that I am location independent and use technology to perform my job, rather than being physically present at my clients' headquarters or offices. This was certainly the case during the height of Covid but as restrictions ended and the world opened up again I have a mixture of digital and face to face assignments, some based in the Caribbean and some based in Europe. I recently returned from a trip to Amsterdam where I was a keynote speaker for International Women's Day on Embracing Equity.

Since relocating to Dominica I have spoken at seven conferences in the UK via Zoom and facilitated management and leadership development programmes using either Microsoft Teams or Zoom for my international clients. I have had to upskill myself to use these platforms and to learn how to engage audiences online, where you can't see body language properly, or pick up on those subtle nuances that tell you if your point is hitting home. I read an article recently where it was suggested you had to have "virtual charisma" to really lock people in and deliver a memorable message online! This is something that I have taken on board and will continue to develop. Moving from ninety percent face to face delivery and ten percent online, to thirty percent face to face and seventy percent online has been a big shift for me. I truly believed that delivering sessions and holding meetings online was not as effective as face to face, however, I have had great feedback from clients that I have been coaching via Zoom, some of whom I have never met in person, and following a recent management development course that I delivered online, a delegate wrote to thank me and said that she had found speaking on Microsoft Teams had increased her confidence and allowed her to voice concerns that she would not normally articulate. This has increased my belief in this way of working and I now offer as standard the option of face to face or online.

My working methodology is that I do not employ staff, instead I bring experts in on a freelance basis as and when required, which means that I can "flex". When my workload is busy, I tap into the bank of freelance consultants from my global network, and when I am quiet, I lie in bed late, chill out and just enjoy life. This is my idea of work life balance and now, if I want to have some time off work, I just tell clients that I am not available for that period of time.

However, to operate as a well-oiled machine it's imperative to have people around you who you can trust to deliver on time and to the same standard and quality that clients have come to expect from you. My team are based all over the world, though mainly in the UK because that is where I originally established my business. There are three key organisations which have worked with me and supported me for many years and which are responsive to my needs. Without their continued support I would face many more challenges! There's the wonderful Ruth Robinson from Brighter Business Solutions, who provides PR and marketing support. I think Ruth can actually read my mind, we are so attuned to one another. Greenlight Computers have been providing my computer support for over twelve years and continue to support me remotely from the UK. And last but not least, Mark Catell from Mawebdesign, who looks after all things website/design related.

In Dominica I am still establishing my network of support and this includes my accountant, Marvlyn Estrado of KPB Chartered Accountants; my legal representative, Noelize Knight Didier, Partner at Harris, Harris & Didier, Attorneys-at-law; and for secretarial support, Kermecia Matthew-Harris, owner of Harmony Virtual Assistance. I am still looking for a Caribbean PR company to help me break into the Caribbean market. Having worked for myself for twenty-five years, I have found that the services of a good PR company have been instrumental to my success. I tend to change them regularly depending on the goals I want to achieve.

The first company was employed to help me win awards and ensure that my business received the necessary accolades to propel my success!

The second company helped me to build my Facebook and LinkedIn profiles, write blogs and creative posts to build my followers.

The third company had a deep knowledge of Twitter and helped to create more posts, and assisted in creating a marketing plan to ensure consistency.

The fourth and last company I still work with now. I employ them on a project basis, for example when launching my book, promoting a training programme, creating content for my website, etc. Unfortunately, they are not familiar with the Caribbean market.

CHAPTER 19
From dream to reality – working in Dominica

There is something very satisfying about working in the country where you were born. Having read this far, you will know that it has not been an easy road to travel and I am not yet at my destination, however, I do have cause to celebrate. I have managed to secure pieces of work in all the areas that I specialise in:

HR/Consultancy

One of my first pieces of work was working in partnership with another consultancy on a HR Gap Analysis for the Government of the Commonwealth of Dominica. This involved communicating with approximately eighty stakeholders and gave me the opportunity to have face to face meetings with many NGO's and public sector organisations. The research was interesting and gave me some insight into the future workforce requirements necessary to build a resilient Dominica, the challenges faced by the government regarding population growth and the need to develop the skills required to meet Dominica's goals and aspirations.

Leadership Development - NBD

The National Bank of Dominica Ltd (NBD) is the leading financial institution in Dominica and has been operating since 1978. The assignment involved delivering my Global Leadership Programme to their Executive Team, Managers and Supervisors. Having previously delivered this programme in over twenty-five countries, it was wonderful to engage with Dominica's current and future leaders. I have been blown away by the passion and enthusiasm for their work. I was fortunate enough to be working with NBD when they took home all five 2022 Bank of the Year Awards at a ceremony held virtually on 15 December with live streaming. Each year the Eastern Caribbean Central Bank (ECCB) recognises the commercial banks operating within the Eastern Caribbean Currency Union (ECCU) for their exceptional banking services and demonstration of social responsibility in their communities.

OLIVE STRACHAN MBE

Leadership Development - Jollys

I was then fortunate enough to work with Jollys Pharmacy Ltd, a family-owned business located in Dominica. It is an innovative pharmacy which opened in 1980 and operates a wholesale centre, manufacturing subsidiary, and fitness centre. They are a leading Caribbean pharmacy which fosters good community health practices through their public health programs and have received the Caribbean Pharmacy Sigma Business Award from the Caribbean Association of Pharmacists. It has been a pleasure to work with the Managers/Supervisors at Jollys, these young leaders prove that the future of dynamic Dominica is in good hands.

Motivational Speaker - Sagicor

Sagicor Life Insurance Company is one of the leading financial services companies in Dominica. First established in 1840, they are the second oldest insurer in the Americas and a market leading provider of insurance products and financial services. I was fortunate to be the keynote speaker at their staff conference. The theme was "Go Brave" and was opened by the indigenous people of Dominica called the Kalinago, who began the event with drums and traditional dancing. It was a high energy, engaging event with every staff member playing their part.

Speaker at the Special Olympics Dominica

Until recently I was not aware of the Special Olympics. This is a global organisation, established in 1968, which serves athletes with intellectual disabilities. They work with thousands of coaches and volunteers every year. I was recently requested by my fellow Rotarian, Desrie Joseph-Elwin, to speak to the athletes as they were preparing to go to the Special Olympic Games in Berlin. It was such a pleasure to speak to these talented people who have a thirst to bring home gold. Their success could not happen without the support of their parents and volunteers, who work tirelessly to provide support and leadership. I felt privileged to be given this opportunity. I am looking forward to hearing the results of their endeavours!

At the time of writing my book, I have sent out proposals and attended meetings with other organisations in Dominica. This is my third year on the island and slowly I can see the fruits of my labour beginning to develop. Every project had given me further insight into the business and professional community in Dominica. Each experience has allowed me to use my skills and grow into my new community and new life. Everyone has been very generous, making me feel welcome and showing appreciation for my efforts.

I often bring neuroscience into my leadership development training; it deals with the structure or function of the nervous system and the brain. Studies in neuroscience encourage us to embrace change and do things differently, as it has been proven that keeping the brain agile delays the aging process. I feel that coming to Dominica and making the long-term changes that I have made, along with working with new clients, learning the cultural norms of Dominica, and building new client relationships, has benefited me enormously.

Lessons learnt

First and foremost are compromise and tolerance. When you first arrive in a new country it is tempting to make constant comparisons, many of them unfavourable because things are different from what you are used to. Dominica has its own pace and rhythm. Just queuing at the bank or going to Digicel or Flow, the two main internet and mobile phone providers, to sort out a problem can take hours of your time. Customer service can vary, from very good to very bad. When you first arrive, you spend a lot of time complaining and your blood pressure goes through the roof. I have learnt to just move to the rhythm and stop railing against it. You can't change it, so just go with it.

The culture is different! Dominica has religion at its heart. Every event I have attended, be it face to face or online, starts with a prayer. When you attend an event, protocol demands that each speaker formally names and addresses each dignitary in the room. This can seem tedious because after you have heard it six times it can get irritating, but this is how things are done and you have to respect the cultural norms. It reminds me of when I worked in the Middle East and I would hear the expression "Inshallah" almost every day, the literal meaning being "If God wills". In Dominica you frequently hear "It's in God's hands", or "To Father be the glory", or "Give God thanks".

It takes time to be accepted. Dominicans have a fierce loyalty to each other and the focus is on buying local and promoting home grown businesses. Infiltrating this market as a relative stranger is difficult. Selling your services takes time. You may visit a potential client feeling that the meeting has gone well but it can take a year before the deal is closed.

The economy is very different. Dominica has many entrepreneurs and a lot of them are micro businesses. It is a small country with a falling birth rate and because it is constantly being impacted by challenging weather conditions it is difficult for businesses to maintain prosperity. Each hurricane or tropical storm can bring the country to its knees and there is a great deal of investment in climate resilience training to help businesses withstand this onslaught. There is not a great deal of foot fall and most people have a full-time job as well as what they call a "side hustle", which brings another income into the household. The government also promotes and supports Dominicans working remotely in other countries.

I have learnt to appreciate Dominica's spectacular scenery and breathtaking beauty. Even after living here for nearly three years, there are areas that we have not yet visited. Every day I feel grateful that I am able to live here. I am convinced that it is benefiting me physically and emotionally.

CHAPTER 20
The next step – professionally speaking

Self-development

TetraMap® is a globally proven model, tool and framework that helps businesses to unlock potential and transform team performance. I have been an accredited TetraMap® Facilitator for over ten years and have used this tool in all aspects of my work, from coaching, delivering training and as a conference speaker. I believe there is a market for TetraMap® in the Caribbean and with this in mind I have invested in becoming a Master Facilitator. When qualified, this will allow me to train others to be Facilitators. I am currently two thirds through the certification and look forward to bringing this excellent tool to the Caribbean in the future.

Coaching and mentoring

Dr Akwi Asombang has very kindly promoted my book to all her contacts, particularly her mentees at The PanAfrican Organisation for Health Education & Research (POHER), an NGO with a focus on the soundness of the health sector as the cornerstone of all African countries. Their goal is to improve health awareness in African communities; promote and advocate the creation of partnership between health professionals in Africa and overseas, irrespective of country or residence; introduce and promote the use of new and adapted technologies in healthcare and education in Africa; and mobilise material resources for healthcare services in Africa.

I have been working with Dr Akwi and the POHER medical scholars providing mentoring and coaching services for the past two years. Because all the students are based in various locations around the world, the sessions are conducted online. It is such a pleasure to work with these medical scholars. It gives me a deep sense of pride and satisfaction as I listen to their goals and aspirations for a career in medicine. Each one of these students wants to make the world a better place and use their training and qualifications to help, heal and create health and wellness in their country and beyond. It is wonderful to sit in my office in

Dominica and coach and mentor students from Cameroon, Sierra Leone, Nigeria, Kenya, Egypt, Ethiopia, and Zambia. These young medical students have inspired me with their pride in their country and their desire to improve the lives of their communities.

Marketing campaign

Having tried radio and book launches to raise my profile in Dominica, I am now planning a marketing campaign to increase my visibility and further establish Olive Strachan Consultancy. I have made contact with the two local papers, The Chronicle and The Sun, and I am working with an organisation to design an eye-catching advertisement. There will be Facebook advertisements, which will also be posted across all my social media platforms, and there will be an email campaign. I will be advertising my Open Programmes which will give organisations the opportunity to send individual Managers/Leaders to my courses.

Growth potential in the Caribbean

The Organisation of Eastern Caribbean States (OECS) is an international inter-governmental organisation dedicated to regional integration in the Eastern Caribbean. The vision of the organisation for 2020-2024 is "A better quality of life for the people of the OECS" and their Mission Statement aims "To drive and support sustainable development through regional integration, collective action and development cooperation."

The Caribbean is renowned as one of the top global tourist destinations, but it is also an attractive place to start a business. Islands including Turks and Caicos, Jamaica, and the Dominican Republic are leading the way, having benefited from strong fiscal growth for the business owners and start up initiatives. I plan to purchase databases for potential islands that could benefit from my business services and market myself there.

I have also held meetings via Zoom with other consultants based in the Caribbean to discuss potential collaborations on future projects.

Leaving a lasting impact

My career in HR/Learning and Development has allowed me to coach, mentor, and train others and over the years I have received positive feedback regarding my impact on others. I have recently been involved in coaching mainly female entrepreneurs. Part of my philosophy is that it is vital that every professional has a social media presence, so I can connect with them outside of our coaching sessions and keep abreast of their achievements and success.

CHAPTER 21
Inspiring Footprints

I am spending a lot of time reflecting this year. Earlier in this book I shared how it has taken time over the years to build my confidence, hone my craft and become an expert in my field, as a result of which I have touched others and imparted and shared my knowledge. Developing others to reach their full potential is something that holds great meaning for me. There are many people in my life who coached and mentored me, opening doors and believing in me.

Part of a life well-lived is the impact you have had on others. To feel your life has not just been a selfish endeavour but that others have benefited from being around you, working with you, or just being your friend.

Over my working life I have coached many people, some men but mainly women. I asked four women that I have been coaching or working with recently to give me a short case study about themselves, our working relationship, the impact I have had, and their plans for the future. You can read all about them in the Appendix.

I avidly follow each of these women on social media, and I am so proud of every one of them. They are intelligent, talented, amazing young women with a wealth of success before them. I am so proud to have had the opportunity help hone their abilities and be a sounding board and support when needed. Every time you coach or mentor someone they bring you into their world. Each of these women have brought something into my life. Learning about their different industries and seeing life through their lens has enriched my life.

CHAPTER 22
Living my prime!

At the time of writing this book I am approaching my sixty-second birthday and feel excited and optimistic about the future. There is a great deal to look forward to. Our son Ricky is marrying his fiancée, Sereyna, in September 2023, in Portugal, a good reason for the whole family to get together. My daughter Rhia and her family are also visiting us in Dominica for the first time - something that Errol and I have dreamed of, that this family home in Dominica becomes a true family home, with our children being regular visitors.

We will put the finishing touches to our Caribbean home, which includes completing the ground floor apartment and seeking the right tenant.

I plan to visit the UK at least once a year and continue to travel for business as well as for recreational purposes.

We are looking forward to our children and grandchildren visiting us on a regular basis and enjoying the delights of the Caribbean.

I will continue to be part of my networking groups, building friendships and getting more involved in the Dominican community.

My husband and I plan to visit all the Caribbean islands over the next twenty years or so, immersing ourselves in the different cultures. I don't see myself retiring, as such, because my life and my work give me joy and purpose.

Recently our friends from the UK have come to visit us in Dominica. A husband-and-wife couple sailed from the Canaries to the Caribbean, visiting Dominica on their travels. We met them in Portsmouth and spent a lovely day having lunch and sightseeing. We then enjoyed drinks on their boat. We have plans to sail with them later in the year to the Grenadines.

The following week Diane and John, friends we have known for thirty years, were on a Caribbean cruise and stopped off in Roseau. Once again we were tour guides for the day, taking them to all our favourite places - Trafalgar Falls, Jungle Bay, and Scott's Head. It was a wonderful experience to share our new home with old friends.

Moments of pure joy!

I am sitting in the garden as I write the final chapters of my book. There is nothing more sublime than waking up in the morning in my Caribbean home, preparing my favourite pure-ground Dominican coffee and sitting down in the shade of the porch to look out on our beautiful garden. During previous visits to the Caribbean, visiting friends or relatives, we would walk through flower filled gardens and there would be dozens of hummingbirds darting around. I would look at their beauty and wish that one day I would have a garden full of verdant lushness, with hummingbirds adding that special energetic colour and light. I have fulfilled my dream.

My eyes roam over the purple, white, orange, and pink bougainvillea, the bright beauty a feast for the eyes. The scent of roses, jasmine, Ylang Ylang and the Rangoon creeper assail my senses. The Flamboyant tree, which sheds all its leaves once a year, leaving bare stumps for a few months giving the impression that the tree has died, suddenly sprouts fresh leaves and becomes bushy again, with beautiful orange flowers. It is the centre piece of the whole garden, providing shade and beauty. My husband's favourites are the hibiscuses, which nod their heads in the gentle breeze in every shade, from white to gorgeous velvety purples and reds. The garden is a perfect combination of our mixed heritage, Dominican and Jamaican. Errol has selected trees that remind him of his childhood and grows those that he enjoys eating.

I am looking out through gaps in the trees, as I sit here. We are surrounded by rich vegetation through which I can see what is happening around me but because of Errol's clever design, I can't be seen. I feel like I am in a safe haven, taking pleasure from my surroundings and feeling the calm sense of appreciation. I know that although I will visit my second home, the UK, on a regular basis, I am living in my final resting place.

CHAPTER 23
Full circle

"To reach your desired destination, the person in charge of the controls must be you"!
Olive Strachan

I feel like I have come full circle in my life, leaving Dominica as a child and returning as a mature woman, starting a new life, and rediscovering who I am. I love the combination of the different pace of life, facing new challenges and creating a life that is fun, varied, and purposeful.

I do sometimes wonder if I should I have returned to the Caribbean earlier. Have I left it too late, starting again at fifty-nine, could I have achieved more? This quote from Ecclesiastes 3:1 resonates with me, "For everything there is a season, and a time for every purpose under heaven."

Returning to the Caribbean with the expertise, qualifications, and knowledge that I have amassed over the years as a global consultant means that I have a great deal to offer. Precisely because I am mature, and comfortable financially, I can be selective as to the type of work I do, and my circle of friends are people who I feel that I have a connection with.

I will not let society limit my success because of my age; I am passionate about my marriage, my children, my grandchildren, and my work. There is so much more that I would like to achieve, maybe the best is yet to come? As long as I can maintain my health and the drive to create new opportunities for myself, I will survive and thrive.

So, when exactly are we in our prime? My conclusion is that being in your prime is a state of mind, whether you are reading this book in your forties, fifties, sixties, and beyond, being able to take advantage of your prime means having the confidence to grasp opportunities that you have created or that present themselves to you.

All too often we look at ourselves through the lens of others. The doubters, the haters who attempt to halt your forward trajectory because by achieving success you emphasise their lack of it. If I had listened to the negative opinion of others, I would never have accomplished so much and be the happy and fulfilled woman I am today.

I will never give up on trying to achieve more, be better than I am, and grow and develop my skills and abilities. As Nelson Mandela said "A winner is a dreamer who never gives up."

The reality is that at sixty, if I am lucky, I have thirty years of life left. I am already making plans for how I can keep my mind and body in peak condition. With this in mind, I recently completed my first hike in twenty years with a hiking group called Dwivayez which has been established for twenty-two years. The hike was from an area of Dominica called Scotts Head and ended at Soufriere. It took five hours and involved climbing a mountain full of fallen tree debris, damp underfoot, so easy to slip and fall. We climbed over rocks, using a rope to leverage ourselves upwards. Many times during the hike I wanted to give up. It was definitely about endurance as well as some level of fitness. I had tremendous support from the more experienced hikers and my husband, who also carried my backpack for me. There was a round of applause when I completed the hike and we finished the day by having a swim in the beautiful Caribbean Sea at Champagne Beach. Dominica is known for its mountainous, rough terrain and the hike was one of the hardest things I have ever experienced, I compare it to giving birth! However, I pushed myself to the limit and am now preparing myself for the next one in a month's time.

It's all about choices. I previously mentioned my health problems, that I was pre-diabetic, had low vitamin D levels which were causing my insomnia, and high blood pressure. I chose to make changes to my diet and to walk for 10,000 steps every night. On a recent visit to my doctor he informed me that I was no longer pre-diabetic and my vitamin D levels were now normal! I was so elated, I nearly hugged him. I made the right choice for me and am now reaping the benefits. My next goal is to get my blood pressure down to normal levels. As Ken Levine said "We all make choices, but in the end our choices make us."

PRIME

My poem below, *Choices,* encourages you to make the right choice for you!

Stop waiting – start doing
Stop watching – get involved
Stop sitting – start moving
Stop hesitating – push forward
Stop asking for permission – take action
Stop silently accepting – use your voice
Stop shrinking to fit – create your own space
Stop negative comparisons – celebrate your uniqueness
Stop feeling like an imposter – step into your power!

I am finishing my book with a quote from Michelle Yeoh, the sixty-year-old, Malaysian-born actor who became the first Asian woman to win the Academy Award for Best Performance by an Actress in a Leading Role in *Everything Everywhere All at Once* at the Oscars on 12 March 2023.

In her speech she said, "For all the little boys and girls who look like me watching tonight, this is a beacon of hope and possibility. This is proof - dream big and dreams do come true. And ladies, don't let anyone ever tell you you're past your prime!"

APPENDIX
Inspiring footprints

I asked four women that I have been coaching or working with recently to give me a short case study about themselves, our working relationship, the impact I have had and their plans for the future. They are intelligent, talented, amazing young women with a wealth of success before them and I am proud to have had the opportunity to work with them.

Every time you coach or mentor someone, they bring you into their world. Working with each of these women has enriched my life.

Dr. Akwi Asombang

Who are you/your business?

I am an Interventional Gastroenterologist at Massachusetts General Hospital, Harvard Medical School, Massachusetts, USA. I am also the Director of the Global Gastroenterology Program at Massachusetts General Hospital. I am the cofounder of the Pan-African Organization for Health, Education and Research (POHER) and the founder of the African Association of future Gastroenterologists (AAFG). POHER is a NGO with a focus on the soundness of the health sector as the cornerstone of social and economic development of all African countries.

POHER goals are to improve health awareness in African communities, promote and advocate the creation of partnership between health professionals in Africa and overseas, irrespective of country of residence, and to introduce and promote the use of new and adapted technologies in healthcare and education in Africa. In addition, we aim to mobilize material resources for healthcare services in Africa.

As POHER, one of our major programs, is focused on mentorship. In the past we mentored students in various careers within the African continent, but more recently we have focused specifically on medical students.

How have you found working with Olive?

I initially worked with Olive several years ago, with the intention of developing and investing into my organization, POHER. I was interested in finding ways to strengthen our board, fundraise and the implementation of the organization's activities. Secondly, I wanted input on personal branding and growth that could positively contribute towards the growth of POHER.

I first heard Olive speaking at a women's meeting hosted by one of my friends, Dr Catherine Muyeba, and I was hooked by the message Olive shared and her infectious laughter. During that initial encounter I found Olive to be very genuine as she described her life and professional experience. I found the questions she asked to be very thought-provoking and led me to reflect on my own priorities. Thus, I set up an initial appointment which led to several more appointments with Olive. I have found discussions with Olive to be very engaging and honest, with her providing constructive feedback. She is prepared for meetings and made sure I was prepared by sharing the agenda and tasks to complete prior to our meetings so that our encounter would be productive. She is a joy to work with and makes every session productive and enjoyable. She listens to your questions and jointly tackles solutions by asking insightful questions. She helped create solutions during the open conversations and follows-up in the next meeting. She provides empowering messages and skills to maximize one's potential. Olive is approachable and resourceful in providing tools for success. It was my interactions with her that led me to establish sessions between her and our POHER mentees over the years. The response from the mentees is extremely positive. Olive helps build confidence and elevate self-esteem.

Has working with Olive Strachan Consultancy helped your business?

Yes, working with Olive has helped me personally and helped my NGO, POHER. Olive has brought more ways for me to think of structure in my personal growth and development. In terms of the organization she has truly made me reflect on our goals and planned activities. Olive provided guidance on organizational restructuring and targets. Her feedback has helped with implementing change with organizational leadership, administrative assistance, and branding. Olive listened to our concerns and questions then returned with actionable tasks to address the challenges. She has helped us focus on time management, branding, networking, and fundraising. Working with Olive Strachan Consultancy has resulted in positive results that include improved communication of planned organization activities. The positive impact Olive has made in my life and for our mentees resulted in us inviting her to speak at our annual POHER Medical Research and Mentorship Conference. Over the past two years I have made it a point for her to meet with each of our POHER mentees. In addition, we have invited her as one of the main speakers at our annual Medical Research and Mentorship Symposium. Having Olive share her experience as a global entrepreneur, author and coach is integral to our medical students as they progress into careers as medical doctors serving the community.

What are your future plans, what's next for you?

My plans involve focusing on methods that can be implemented to raise awareness about POHER and raise the support needed to grow as an organization. As an individual, I have benefited from Olive as a consultant, but we have also developed an enriching friendship. I can call/text/email Olive as a friend. As POHER, we have ideas and programs that will provide mentorship for more individuals and positively impact our communities. We are exploring organizational structure that includes empowering our board members and maintaining the diversity in leadership. In addition, we are exploring POHER organizational committees with action items over the course of the year. POHER has received an increase in requests for participation as mentees or involvement as volunteers. One of the key questions that remains is how do we obtain and sustain financial stability to continue with our POHER organization goals? Our POHER programs are needed and greatly impact individuals and communities. We aim to continue working with Olive as we strengthen our organization.

Lizra Fabien

Who are you/your business?

I am a global citizen as well as a Private Sector development professional, having worked with and represented the private sector locally, regionally and globally. I have recently transitioned from my six-year experience as the Executive Director of the Dominica Association of Industry and Commerce, the local Chamber of Commerce. I am currently managing a Women's Economic Empowerment project across the Caribbean, as well as being the Founder of *The Progressive Mind* which was designed to enhance the lives of professionals and entrepreneurs.

How have you found working with Olive?

Working with Olive has made a marked improvement in my professional experience. I think that Olive has the perfect combination of energy, experience, insight, and understanding, which means that there has been no dull moment, always laughter, smiles and careful thought. There is no replacement for Olive in my experience and I have been better for Olive having moved to Dominica when she did. Olive's openness in thought and willingness to continue to learn and enhance her skills in order to continue to be globally relevant has been a catalyst to our good working relationship.

Has working with Olive Strachan Consultancy helped your business?

In my work with the Chamber, Olive brought her energy, suggestions and value as a member, and even more so when she became one of my Board members. On a personal side, Olive has been a voice of reason to motivate me professionally. I was pleased and grateful when Olive supported Progressism, my annual event for professionals in Dominica, and brought inspiration to the attendees as the keynote speaker of the first physically hosted edition.

What are your future plans, what's next for you?

I aim to continue to increase my impact across the region and globally with businesses, professionals and women. Specific to my brand, The Progressive Mind, I aim to continue delivering relevant value to my customers through products and experiences. In the not-too-distant future, I look forward to collaborating with Olive in delivering some value products we have discussed. The future is bright so I believe that despite the challenges ahead, the best is still yet to come and my prime is ahead!

Samantha Lubanzu

Who are you/your business?

I currently hold the volunteer appointment of Vice-Chair & Inclusion & Diversity Lead of the CIPD in Manchester, UK. I am also recognised amongst my peers as the top DEI coach in Manchester, UK, and am a top eighty Neurodiversity evangelist.

With my skills to teach and train people, I empower them to bring transformational changes in their personal and professional lives. I strive in particular to empower and build confidence in women of colour and allies through my online transformational programs which enable them to progress and move up the career ladder to senior-level roles or accelerate in their businesses. My vision is to assist them in emerging as successful and valued professional women and still enjoy a balanced home and family life.

My Mission is to help one million businesses to truly represent the diverse world we live in and in doing so have long term organisational success.

OLIVE STRACHAN MBE

How have you found working with Olive?

Working with Olive has been an incredibly inspirational experience. She is a force of nature who continuously encourages and motivates me and so many others to strive for excellence and reach our full potential. I have had the opportunity to learn from Olive, and through her guidance I've been able to create a better future for myself. Olive is a role model and an example of how hard work, dedication and passion can lead to success.

I'm so grateful to have Olive in my life and I'm very fortunate to have the chance to collaborate with her. She's an amazing woman and a true inspiration. I'm so proud to be part of her journey and can't wait to see what the future holds!

Has working with Olive Strachan Consultancy helped your business?

Working with Olive Strachan Consultancy has been an incredibly inspirational experience for both me and my business, providing me with the guidance and support I needed to make transformational strides in my business. With her expertise I have been able to create tangible goals and results for both myself and my business. I am truly grateful for all Olive has done and would highly recommend Olive Strachan Consultancy for anyone seeking to make real positive change in their business. Together, we have made great strides towards success.

What are your future plans, what's next for you?

My future plans are to build on my success and continue to help empower other women and people of colour in business and career. I want to create a pathway for them to break through the six-figure income bracket while still having work-life balance. Ultimately, I aim to be a driving force behind creating an inclusive business world where everyone has equal opportunity. As we all know, diversity is key to success. I'm looking forward to utilising my insights and experiences to make a positive impact on the business world. There's no denying that together we can achieve great things.

Through this work, I want to continue to embolden and inspire other women and people of colour so they too can find success. I'm passionate about creating a better future and making sure no one is left behind. Now more than ever, it's important that we come together to ensure everyone has the opportunity to reach their potential and create a brighter future for us all.

It's going to take hard work but I'm confident that my efforts will help pave the way. I'm ready to turbo-charge the success of others and make sure that everyone has access to the same opportunities. It's time for us to come together and create a more equitable world where we can all thrive.

In addition to my consulting work, I'm also looking forward to continuing my work in the community. Whether through mentorship, advocacy or volunteering,

I know there's still much more that can be done to improve our communities and I'm ready to do my part.

I'm excited for what the future holds and am confident that together we can create a world where everyone has equal opportunities and can find success.

Let's all work together to create a more equitable, diverse and inclusive world—one where everyone has the chance to thrive. I'm ready for what's next and once again so happy that Olive is on my business journey!

Martina Witter

Who are you/your business?

Martina Witter is a Director of award-winning Rapha Therapy & Training Services (established in 2014), Accredited Cognitive Behaviour Therapist, Mindset Coach, Health & Wellbeing Consultant, Author, Podcast Host (Rivers to Resilience), Blogger, Resilience Expert, Founder of Black Mental Wealth and Cofounder of Black Women in Business and Professionals Network. Martina has over twenty years' experience working within the wellbeing and mental health field, helping diverse individuals (children, adolescents and adults) to develop a strong mindset that allows them to turn bottlenecks into breakthroughs, increase performance and productivity in organizations. Due to her contributions to the field, she has been featured in HuffPost, Thrive Global, Metro, The Voice, and BBC Radio Manchester. Martina delivers transformational, dynamic and experiential training whilst also having a passion to see individuals thrive holistically in life through being revived, restored and refocused. Martina delivers coaching and psychological therapy in innovative and accessible ways including online (video & instant messaging) and via telephone. Martina draws upon her life experiences including bereavements, rejection and stress to connect and empathize with her clients whilst sharing how she has successfully navigated adversity and utilized this for transformation and growth. Martina has a passion for business, inclusivity and collaboration which is evident through Black Mental Wealth, a platform for Black and mixed heritage individuals which challenges the mental health stigma and raises awareness of mental health along with culturally appropriate solutions, and Black Women in Business and Professionals Network (BWIBP), which improves opportunities for career and business growth through expanding networks and creating access to Black female role models. BWIBP runs quarterly networking events in Manchester, hosting stellar business leaders and professionals as speakers whilst also creating a community for Black women to grow and raise awareness of local and national resources and events that can facilitate this.

How have you found working with Olive?

Working with Olive has been a pleasure as she is warm, engaging and adapts her coaching style to the individual. I thrived working with Olive as she is high energy, inspirational and empowering whilst encouraging, which allowed me to take action to increase my business sales, visibility, strengthen my brand position, personal branding and credibility. Olive allowed me to see beyond my current business accomplishment whilst guiding me in celebrating the growth journey whilst successfully navigating setbacks. Olive consistently provided constructive feedback which facilitated me in gaining clarity regarding my business goals and gaining optimal outcomes.

Has working with Olive Strachan Consultancy helped your business?

Yes, it has definitely helped with business growth and implementing systems and structures that will ensure business efficiency and growth. It has increased my confidence as a director in running a consultancy and I have greater clarity regarding what aspects of the business should be prioritized for growth. It allowed me to consider business development opportunities and planning for growth regarding human resources. I have developed my leadership skills including critical thinking, decision making, adaptability and relationship building.

What are your future plans, what's next for you?

Recruiting associate training facilitators; delivering Power Hour Wellbeing Workshops to schools, colleges, universities and corporate; delivering Confidence Coaching for Women; and developing a Wellbeing App.

Dr. Catherine Sampa Muyeba

Who are you/your business?

I am a Regional Lead Consultant Psychiatrist with over twenty years of clinical experience in the community, hospitals, prisons and the private sector. I support adults, children and families affected by substance misuse, with or without mental illness. I have a special interest in the assessment, treatment and research in attention deficit hyperactivity disorder (ADHD) in adults and run a private clinic in Manchester.

I teach medical students and psychiatry trainees, as well as clinicians and health professionals in other disciplines. A Certified Lifestyle Physician and international speaker, I coach, mentor, educate, and raise awareness about mental health, addictions, and lifestyle medicine with a view to reducing stigma, improving help-seeking and promoting total wellbeing among professionals and the communities they serve.

I founded REAPing Women, an inspiring movement dedicated to helping every woman become their best self so that they can enrich their lives and make a positive impact in the world. REAPing is a lifestyle that promotes regular Reflection, Envisioning, Action-Planning, Enjoying and Reviewing life. This health and wellness coaching business provides personalised coaching sessions and group coaching programmes to enable women worldwide to make sustainable lifestyle changes that lead to long-term health benefits.

I am involved with various community activities including leadership in the Zambia Overseas Christian Fellowship charity, and a Trustee at the Homes of Hope charity.

I have been married to Maybin for over 30 years and have two adult children, Cynthia and Daniel. I am actively involved in pastoral care at my local church in Manchester. In my spare time, I organise kitchen parties, baby showers and networking events. I also design for my online clothing line, Chitenge Garments.

How have you found working with Olive?

I first met Olive just before the Covid 19 pandemic in 2020 when she spoke at a networking event. I have had the privilege of working with her since then and she has been instrumental in helping me achieve my personal and professional goals. I believe that the insights gained from our coaching sessions will continue to benefit me in the future. She has also spoken at my events and thoroughly inspired my community.

Professionalism: From the outset, Olive has demonstrated a high degree of professionalism in her approach. She is always punctual, well-prepared, and focused during sessions. I found this level of professionalism very reassuring and it helped me to build trust and confidence in the coaching process.

Insightful: One of the things that impressed me the most about Olive is her ability to ask insightful questions that helped me gain a deeper understanding of my strengths and areas of development. She has a natural ability to listen actively and provide guidance that is relevant and practical. Through her coaching, I was able to identify my goals, develop a clear vision of what I wanted to achieve in my business and create actionable plans to get there.

Accountability: Another aspect of working with Olive was the accountability factor. She has held me accountable for the actions I committed to, which motivated me to take consistent and purposeful action towards my goals. This accountability was a crucial element in my success and it helped me to stay focused and motivated throughout the coaching process. She inspired me to write my first book!

Encouraging: Olive is very encouraging and a tremendous source of support for me. She provided positive feedback and helped me to recognise my achievements, which boosted my confidence and self-belief. The guidance and encouragement made the coaching process very enjoyable and rewarding.

In conclusion, I am grateful for the opportunity to have worked with Olive and believe that the insights gained through our coaching sessions will continue to benefit me in the future. I would highly recommend coaching to anyone who wants to achieve their full potential and reach their goals.

Has working with Olive Strachan Consultancy helped your business?

Definitely! Working with the Olive Strachan consultancy was a positive experience for my business. Her expertise, fresh perspective, customised solutions, and ability to improve my performance were instrumental in helping me to overcome challenges and achieve my business goals.

What are your future plans, what's next for you?

To start with, I want to prioritise the publication of my book and produce the accompanying online course. I will be developing new programmes and focus on expanding my reach as I get feedback from the women I serve.

My goal is to continue growing my coaching and speaking business by providing value to my clients and building strong relationships with them. I will consistently deliver high-quality services, building trust, and establish a strong reputation worldwide.

ACKNOWLEDGEMENTS

I would like to thank the following people:

My husband Errol Strachan for being there at my side for the past forty-two years, providing love and support. Without you this book would not be possible because, although it is the story of my life, it is also about the life we built together. I am looking forward to sharing many more years with you and having many adventures in our new Caribbean home.

To Candace Edwards, our friendship spans over thirty years. As someone who knows me very well, your valuable input in shaping this book is much appreciated. I am so pleased that you were able to proofread and edit my book; your dedication, professionalism, and attention to detail have played a key part in getting this book published.

My daughter Rhia, for writing the Forward to my book, your words are insightful and beautiful. I also appreciate your advice and suggestions; I know that the book is richer and more detailed following your input.

Ruth Robinson, for reading one of the first drafts of my book, your feedback was extremely useful, allowing me to view my book from a different perspective. Ruth and her team will also be responsible for marketing my book and I look forward to collaborating with her again.

Lizra Fabien, who also agreed to give me feedback on the first draft of my book. Lizra gave me a different viewpoint and shared some great ideas, which I implemented.

Lincoln Riviere of Medialinx Studio, for taking the cover photo. I feel the picture epitomises the message behind my book - that you can look good and feel good at any age!

Mark Cattell of Mawebdesign Ltd. Mark was able to use the picture taken by Lincoln to create a fabulous cover for my book.

OLIVE STRACHAN MBE

ABOUT THE AUTHOR

Global business woman, entrepreneur and founder of Olive Strachan Consultancy, ex-Chair of CIPD and CIPD Chartered Companion. Having worked with a variety of Blue-Chip organisations through her career, Olive has spent over twenty-five years developing managers and leaders across the world.

Awarded an MBE by King Charles for her contribution to Business Services and Exporting. The Winner of the Enterprise Vision Awards (EVA) for Training and Coaching. Becoming a Chartered Companion of the CIPD in 2021, one of the highest levels of recognition in the world of HR and people development.

SPEAKER: Guest Speaker | Conference Presenter | Diversity & Inclusion Speaker

COACH: 1:1 Executive and management coaching for business and personal growth helping you gain motivation, confidence, perspective, and work life balance.

CONSULTANT: Design and deliver bespoke programmes on leadership development, performance appraisal and change management.

TRAINER: Expert leadership and management trainer delivering innovative training to develop effective business leaders.

Board Director of Dominica Association of Industry and Commerce (DAIC) and Club Trainer of the Rotary Club of Dominica.

SPECIALITIES: L&D | Leadership Development | SME Growth | Managing Performance | Performance Appraisal | Women in Business | Diversity & Inclusion

OLIVE STRACHAN MBE

OLIVE STRACHAN CONSULTANCY

Olive Strachan MBE, ChCCIPD, MSc (HRM)
Management Development | Performance Improvement | Career Coaching
Bringing you inspiring, engaging and passionate training, that delivers business benefits!

Contact us: +1 767 275 5840

Email: info@olivestrachan.com
Website: www.olivestrachan.com

LinkedIn: https://www.linkedin.com/in/olivestrachan/
Facebook: https://www.facebook.com/OliveStrachanTraining/
Instagram: https://www.instagram/olivestrachan/
Twitter: https://twitter.com/olivestrachan/

Printed in Great Britain
by Amazon